KU-076-264

The
All Electric
Cook
Book

Produced and Published by Spectator Publications Limited

Credits

Contents

Photography by Bryce Attwell

We should like to thank the following
companies for lending or providing
articles for photography.

Asprey & Company Limited
165 New Bond Street, W1

Boadicea British Crafts Shop
19 Beauchamp Place, SW3

Casa Pupo(Artesania Limited)
56 Pimlico Road, SW1

Elizabeth David Limited
46 Bourne Street, SW1

Robert Carrier Cookshop
82 Pimlico Road, SW1

Habitat Limited
77/79 Fulham Road, SW1

Harvey Nichols & Company Limited
Knightsbridge, SW1

Reject China Shop
33 Beauchamp Place, SW3

Robinson & Cleaver Limited
158 Regent Street, W1

Tilemart Limited
151 Great Portland Street, W1

Printed by Hunt Barnard Web Offset Ltd
Aylesbury Bucks

Copyright © 1976 'The All Electric
Cookbook' by Spectator Publications
Limited, London. All rights reserved.
No part of this book may be reproduced
in any form, stored in a retrievable
system, or transmitted in any form or
by any means, electronic, mechanical,
photocopying, recording or otherwise,
without the prior written permission of
the publisher.

Fish

top Fish kebabs
bottom Soused herrings
opposite Grilled mackerel,
and Shellfish risotto

Baking

Whole fish or cutlets and fillets can be baked, with or without liquid.

Thick fish

Whole fish and thick cutlets, such as haddock, cod, mackerel, salmon, and trout.
Clean and wash the fish. Dry well, and season with salt and pepper. Place in greased baking tin with butter or a little liquid. If not using liquid, cover the pan with greased foil. Cook for about 5 minutes per lb at 375°F (190°C).

Thin fish

Fillets of cod or haddock, and whole or filleted flat fish such as plaice or sole.
Clean and prepare as for thick fish. Cook for about 3 minutes per lb at 375°F (190°C).

Frying

There are two methods of frying fish :
1 floured and shallow fried.
2 battered and deep fried.
Method 1
Use for fillets, and small whole fish such as sprats and whitebait.
Wash and dry fish.
Coat with seasoned flour.
Dip in beaten egg then again in flour.
NB The second coating can be of breadcrumbs, instead of flour.
Method 2
Use for large fillets such as cod and haddock.
Wash and dry the fish.
Coat with batter (see page 48).
Lower gently into hot deep fat. Drain on kitchen paper.

Points to remember

☐ The fish must be completely coated to prevent it becoming soggy.
☐ The fat must be at the correct temperature. Test for this by dropping a piece of bread into the fat. If it rises within 30 seconds, the fat is hot enough. If it takes much longer, continue to heat the fat until it reaches the required temperature.
☐ Use only a deep fat fryer and basket when deep frying. Fill only $\frac{1}{3}$ full.
☐ Never leave the pan unattended whilst the fat is heating up.
☐ If fat catches fire turn off the heat immediately and cover the pan with a large plate or special asbestos cloth to exclude air.

What went wrong and why

☐ Food uncooked in centre, but burned on outside – fat too hot, not cooked long enough.
☐ Food and coating soggy – fat too cool.
☐ Coating parting from fish – fish too wet before coating.
☐ Fish tough – fat too cool and too much cooking.
☐ Coating insipid in colour – fat temperature not maintained during cooking.

Grilling

Any sort of fish can be grilled.
Preheat grill to maximum heat. Prepare fish as for baked fish. Brush each fish or piece of fish with melted butter, and place in the grill pan itself, not on the rack, (except for kebabs). Grill *thin fish* for about 7 minutes, turning once during cooking. Grill *thick fish* for about 15 minutes, turning after 10 minutes. Reduce the temperature after about 5 minutes to medium heat. Serve plain grilled fish with *Parsley sauce* (see page 33) or *Maître d' hôtel butter* (see page 9).

Poaching

Use cutlets, fillets or small whole fish such as plaice and sole.
Prepare fish and place in cold liquid such as milk, fish stock or water. Seasonings and flavourings can be

added such as lemon, parsley, bay leaves, onion or peppercorns.
Bring the liquid gently to the boil, and then reduce the heat. Cover the pan and simmer for about 5-10 minutes, depending on the thickness of the fish. To test for readiness, gently part the flakes with a round bladed knife. The fish should have 'set', and should be tender, but not soft.
Lift the fish out from the liquid with a fish slice or draining spoon.

Boiling
Use for large pieces of fish such as salmon or cod.
The term 'boiling' is misleading, as the liquid should never actually boil, but just simmer.
See *Boiled salmon with cucumber sauce* (page 13).

Steaming
Use any small piece of fish or small whole fish.
Prepare as for baked fish. Place in buttered plate and season the fish well with salt and pepper.
Either brush the fish with butter, or place small dots over the top. Add a little liquid and cover the fish with greased foil or greaseproof paper. Place the plate over a saucepan of boiling water or in the top part of a steamer.
Cover and cook gently for about 5-10 minutes depending on the thickness of the fish.

Serving suggestions for fish
Simplicity should be the rule for garnishing fish. Lemon wedges, parsley sprigs, tomato waterlilies or orange slices are ideal.
If sauces are required try cheese or shrimp (see page 33) with white fish. For oily fish, try *Maître d' hôtel butter* (right).

Maître d' hôtel butter
Beat 1 oz butter, 1 tsp chopped parsley and 1 tsp lemon juice together until evenly blended. Roll into a sausage between two sheets of greaseproof paper and leave in the refrigerator to harden. Cut into rounds just before use and place a round on each piece of fish.

Haddock au gratin

Serves 2-3

1	1	medium sized smoked haddock
½ pint	250 ml	white sauce
2 oz	50 g	Cheddar cheese
2	2	tomatoes
1 oz	25 g	butter
1 Tbs	1 Tbs	fresh white breadcrumbs

Preparation time about 20 min
Cooking time 10 min
Poach the haddock in shallow water for 5 minutes. Drain, remove the skin, and flake the fish.
Make up the sauce as directed on page 33 using half milk and half the fish liquid. Add the fish and cheese, mix well and heat through.
Cover the tomatoes with boiling water, leave for a few seconds, drain and remove the skins. Slice thinly and fry them gently in half the butter.
Put half the fish mixture into a shallow ovenproof dish and cover with the tomatoes. Top with the remaining fish mixture and sprinkle with breadcrumbs.
Dot with the remaining butter and grill for 5 minutes.

Tip: To remove the skin easily from the fish before it is cooked, slip it under a hot grill for a few seconds.

Variation: Use sliced mushrooms instead of tomatoes.

Sole bonne femme

Serves 4

8	8	fillets of sole
1	1	shallot
1	1	sprig parsley
2 oz	50 g	mushrooms
1 oz	25 g	butter
2 tsp	2 tsp	plain flour
1	1	egg yolk
2-3 Tbs	2-3 Tbs	cream or top of milk

Garnish

1 Tbs	1 Tbs	chopped parsley

Preparation time about 25 min
Cooking time 40 min
Skin the fish.
Put the skin into a pan with the peeled shallot, parsley sprig, and salt and pepper. Cover with cold water, bring slowly to the boil and simmer for 20 minutes.
Strain the stock into a shallow pan and boil fast until reduced to ½ pint (250 ml).
Fold the fillets in half, season well with salt and pepper and lower into the stock.
Wash and thinly slice the mushrooms, add to the pan with the fish and simmer gently for 10 minutes or until the fish looks opaque. Lift the fish and the mushrooms out and keep hot.
Melt the butter in a small pan, add the flour and mix well. Cook for 2-3 minutes. Remove the pan from the heat and gradually add the fish stock. Bring to the boil, stirring until thickened. Cook for 2-3 minutes.
Remove the pan from the heat and beat in the egg yolk and cream or top of the milk. Do not reboil.
Arrange the fish on a serving dish, top with the mushrooms, and coat with the sauce.
Sprinkle with the chopped parsley and grill for 2-3 minutes.

Variations 1: Sole veronique. Use peeled and pipped grapes instead of mushrooms.
2: Sole mornay. Omit mushrooms and add 1 Tbs Parmesan cheese and 2 oz (50 g) grated Cheddar cheese to the sauce.
3: Sole Florentine. Arrange the cooked fish on a bed of cooked spinach, add 2 oz (50 g) grated cheese to the sauce and pour over the fish. Grill until browned.

Mackerel with caper sauce

Serves 4

4	4	medium sized mackerel
1	1	orange
½ tsp	½ tsp	black pepper
1 pint	500 ml	caper sauce (see page 33)

Preparation time about 10 min
Cooking time 10 min
Wash and scale the fish. Remove the heads and entrails. Wash the insides well with salted water, and dry thoroughly.
Make 2 or 3 small cuts across one side of each fish and brush with oil or melted butter. Place in the grill pan with the rack in the 'down' position.
Cut the orange into four slices, place a slice on each fish and season well with the black pepper. Grill for 10 minutes, turning the fish after 5-7 minutes.
Heat the sauce, adding more salt if necessary.
Arrange the fish on a hot serving dish and serve the sauce separately.

Tip: To grill flat fish such as sole or plaice, brush liberally with butter or margarine and sprinkle with salt and pepper on both sides.

Variations 1: Use lemon and chopped parsley instead of orange for flavour.
2: Use herrings instead of mackerel.

above Boiled salmon
with cucumber sauce
right Sole bonne femme

Soused herrings

Serves 4

8	8	small herrings
½ pint	250 ml	malt vinegar
½ pint	250 ml	water
1	1	cube of sugar
1 tsp	1 tsp	Worcester sauce
1	1	bay leaf
½ tsp	½ tsp	salt

Ovenproof dish 3 in. deep
Preparation time about 10 min
Cooking time 45 min 350°F (180°C)
Wash and scale the fish and cut off the heads. Make a slit along the belly of each from the head end to the tail, and remove the entrails. Wash well.
Place each fish cut side down on a board, and press your knuckles along the backbone. Turn fish over and lift out bone. Leave tail intact.
Mix remaining ingredients together and pour into the dish.
Roll each fish from head to tail and arrange in dish with tails upstanding.
Cover with greased foil and bake in the centre of the oven for 45 minutes.
Serve cold with salad.

Variation: Use mackerel instead of herrings and add 1 orange, sliced, to the liquid.

Stuffed fish

Serves 6

2 lb	1 kg	whole haddock
8 oz	200 g	forcemeat
1	1	large onion
2	2	tomatoes
¼ pint	125 ml	fish stock or water

Preparation time about 20 min.
Cooking time 30 min 375°F (190°C)
Wash and scale the fish, remove the entrails but not the head. Wash well.
Make up the forcemeat as described

on page 36 and pack loosely into the body of the fish ; secure with string or cocktail sticks.
Peel and thinly slice the onion ; slice the tomato and put both into a roasting tin. Place the fish on top of the vegetables with the cut side down.
Season well with salt and pepper ; add the stock and cover the tin with greased foil.
Bake in centre of the oven for 30 minutes.
Serve hot with plain boiled rice.

Tip: Use the vegetables and remaining liquid for soup. Sieve or liquidise the vegetables, add more stock to make up to 1 pint and thicken with 1 Tbs flour mixed to a smooth paste with water. Season well and cook for 10 minutes.

Shellfish risotto

Serves 4

2	2	onions
1	1	clove of garlic
3 Tbs	3 Tbs	oil
1	1	green pepper
6 oz	150 g	long grain rice
1	1	lemon
1 Tbs	1 Tbs	chopped parsley
4 oz	100 g	peeled prawns
1 pint	500 ml	mussels
7 oz	175 g	can of crabmeat

Preparation time about 20 min
Cooking time 30 min
Peel and finely chop the onions and garlic. Fry for 5 minutes in the oil until the onion is transparent. Remove from the pan.
Add rice to remaining oil and fry for 5 minutes or until all the oil has been absorbed. Add the rind and juice of the lemon with the vegetables and parsley, mix well, and cover with cold water.
Bring to the boil, reduce the heat and simmer for 20 minutes or until the

water has been absorbed.
Season well with salt and pepper, add the prawns and mix well.
Scrub the mussels, put into another pan and just cover with water.
Bring to the boil, cover the pan tightly and cook for 2-3 minutes or until the shells are open. Drain and remove some of the mussels from their shells.
Add to the rice with the drained crabmeat. Mix well and heat through.
Serve sprinkled with more fresh parsley.

Fish kebabs

Serves 4

2	2	plaice, filleted
2 oz	50 g	peeled prawns
4	4	scallops
1 tsp	1 tsp	mixed herbs
1	1	lemon
1 Tbs	1 Tbs	soy sauce
a few drops		Tabasco sauce
1 tsp	1 tsp	salt
1	1	clove of garlic
1	1	small onion
4 Tbs	4 Tbs	oil

4 barbecue skewers
Preparation time about 20 min, excluding marinading time
Cooking time 5 min
Cut each fillet in half lengthwise, season well with salt and black pepper. Wrap one or two prawns in each piece of plaice fillet and put into a shallow dish.
Cut each of the scallops in half and mix with the plaice rolls.
Mix together the herbs, rind and juice of the lemon, soy and Tabasco sauces, and salt.
Crush the garlic and finely chop or mince the onion, mix with the oil and pour over the fish. Cover the dish and leave for 2 hours, turning the fish often in the marinade.

Thread the plaice and scallops alternately on fine skewers and grill for 5 minutes or until golden.
Serve with plain boiled rice and green salad.

Boiled salmon with cucumber sauce

Serves 6

2 lb	1 kg	piece of salmon
3½ pints	2 litres	chicken stock
1	1	small cucumber
½	½	lemon
½ oz	15 g	butter
½ oz	15 g	plain flour
1 pint	125 ml	milk
2 Tbs	2 Tbs	cream or top of the milk

Preparation time about 20 min
Cooking time 25 min
Poach the salmon in the court bouillon for 20 minutes.
Peel the cucumber and chop roughly, cover with cold water and bring gently to the boil. Strain off ¼ pint of the liquid and reserve for the sauce.
Press the cucumber through a fine sieve and measure out ¼ pint. Mix with the cucumber liquid.
Melt the butter and add the flour, mix well and cook over a gentle heat for 2-3 minutes. Remove the pan from the heat and gradually add the milk, bring back to the boil, stirring until slightly thickened. Add the cucumber mixture to the sauce and mix well.
Drain the salmon, remove the skin, separate into portions and put onto a serving dish.
Add the cream or top of the milk to the sauce, check the seasoning, and serve with the salmon. Garnish with lemon wedges.

Meat

The cooking times and temperatures given with these recipes are intended only as a guide. Experience will show whether your tastes require slight adjustments to the length of time or degree of heat required.

top Liver pâté
bottom Beef stew
opposite top Roast lamb
opposite bottom Mutton curry,
and Mixed grill

We believe that 350°F (180°C) is the best temperature to roast meat, but the cooking times and oven temperatures are shown here simply as a guide, since the results of roasted meats depend on so many factors. You may prefer only well done beef, in which case the cooking time or oven temperature must be increased. If very rare meat is required, the cooking time will be reduced except when cooking coarse cuts, since these, because of their tougher nature, require long, slow cooking anyway and are thus always eaten well done.

If you use frozen, boneless meat, it must be completely defrosted and allowed to reach room temperature before it is cooked.

Some of the coarse cuts are very lean and it is often a good idea to add extra fat. Lard, dripping or beef suet add to the succulence and flavour of the cooked meat.

Roasting times chart

Beef
at 375°F (190°C)
Rare
Prime joints such as sirloin and whole fillet.
Up to 5 lbs – 15 min per lb plus
15 min over
Over 5 lbs – 15 min per lb : no extra
time added.
At 350°F (180°C)
Medium
Medium cuts such as topside and rib
Up to 5 lbs – 20 min per lb plus
20 min over
Over 5 lbs – 20 min per lb : no extra
time added.
At 350°F (180°C)
Well done
Coarse cuts such as silverside, brisket and flank
Up to 5 lbs – 25-30 min per lb plus
25 min over

Over 5 lbs – 25-30 min per lb : no
extra time added.

Lamb
at 350°F (180°C)
Pink
Thin joints such as shoulder and best end of neck
15 min per lb plus 15 min over
Thick joints such as leg of lamb or mutton
20 min per lb.
Blue (well done)
Thin joints
20 min per lb plus 20 min over
Thick joints
25 min per lb plus 25 min over

Pork and Veal
at 350°F (180°C)
30 min per lb plus 30 min over
Pork must always be thoroughly cooked, so overcook, rather than under-cook. If frozen, make absolutely sure the joint is completely defrosted before cooking.

NB Roast all meats low down in the oven, in the roasting tin provided with the cooker. But remember that, when cooking a full meal, it is often necessary to alter the position of the tin in order to accommodate the other dishes.

Stewing
Used for cooking small pieces of meat or poultry in a quantity of liquid, either on a boiling plate or in the oven.
The meat is cut into even sized pieces, seasoned with salt and pepper and tossed in plain flour.
It is usually browned first in hot fat to seal the outside. It is an ideal method for using cheaper, tough cuts of meat as the long cooking time in liquid renders it tender.

Baking
Ideal for large pieces of meat such as

shoulder and leg of lamb, large cuts of beef, topside, or sirloin.
Meat baked in the oven is usually roasted.
Wipe the meat with a damp cloth and season well with salt and pepper.
Seal the outside of the meat in hot fat, melted in the roasting pan.
See Roasting times chart for cooking times.

Accompaniments to roast beef

Beef
Thin gravy
Strain off the fat.
Add water or vegetable stock to the residue in the pan, stir briskly to blend in with the juices in the pan, and bring to the boil.
Strain into a gravy boat.
Thick gravy
Pour off all but 1 Tbs fat.
Add 1 Tbs plain flour, salt and pepper.
Mix well and cook for about 5 minutes stirring frequently until browned.
Remove the pan from the heat and gradually add water or vegetable stock.
Bring to the boil, stirring until slightly thickened.
Strain into a gravy boat.
Horseradish sauce (see page 35).
NB Ready prepared grated horseradish is an excellent standby for the storecupboard.

Accompaniments to roast pork

Thick and thin gravy are made as for beef (see above).
Apple sauce. Peel and core 1 lb (400 g) of cooking apples and put into a pan with just enough water to cover the base. Simmer for 5 minutes until the apples have pulped. Beat in 1 oz (25 g) castor sugar and 1 Tbs malt vinegar.
Sour cream sauce (see Pork fillets with sour cream sauce page 21).

Accompaniments to roast lamb

Thick and thin gravy are made as for beef (see left).
Mint sauce (see page 33).
Redcurrant sauce Redcurrant jelly can be served on its own or heated gently until liquid and mixed with the same quantity of port wine.
Caper sauce (see page 33).
Espagnole sauce (see page 32).

Beef stew

Serves 4
1 lb	400 g	stewing beef
1 Tbs	1 Tbs	plain flour
1 oz	25 g	dripping or oil
3	3	carrots
1	1	small turnip
2	2	onions
1 pint	500 ml	stock or water

Preparation time about 20 min
Cooking time 2 hours 45 min
Wipe the meat and cut into small pieces.
Season the flour well with salt and pepper. Toss the meat in it to coat completely.
Heat the dripping or oil and fry the meat for 10 minutes, turning it often to brown all over. Remove from the pan.
Scrub and slice the carrots ; thickly peel and dice the turnip ; peel and slice the onions. Fry the vegetables gently in the dripping for 5 minutes. Add the meat, and stock or water. Bring to the boil, season well with salt and pepper. Cover the pan with a tight fitting lid and simmer for 2½ hours.

Variation: Add 1 Tbs tomato purée to the stock or water.

Mutton curry

Serves 4

1 lb	400 g	leg of mutton
1 oz	25 g	dripping or oil
2	2	onions
1	1	small cooking apple
2 tsp	2 tsp	curry powder
1	1	tomato
1 tsp	1 tsp	tomato purée
a pinch of		cinnamon
1	1	bay leaf
2 Tbs	2 Tbs	chutney
2 tsp	2 tsp	redcurrant jelly
a pinch of		cayenne pepper
$\frac{1}{2}$ pint	250 ml	water

Preparation time about 25 min
Cooking time 2$\frac{3}{4}$ hours – 3 hours
Wipe the meat and cut into small
pieces ; season well with salt and
pepper.
Heat the dripping or oil and fry the
meat for 10 minutes, turning it often to
brown all over. Remove it from the pan.
Peel and slice the onions and the
apple ; add both to the remaining
dripping and fry gently for 5 minutes.
Stir in the curry powder and cook for
10 minutes, stirring often to prevent it
burning.
Peel the tomato, halve and remove the
pips. Chop the flesh finely. Add to the
pan with the tomato purée and the
remaining ingredients, except the
water. Mix well.
Remove the pan from the heat and
gradually stir in the water. Bring to the
boil, stirring all the time until slightly
thickened.
Return the meat to the pan, cover and
simmer for 2 - 2$\frac{1}{2}$ hours.
Serve with plain boiled rice.

Tip: Stir the sauce often during the
2 hours cooking period to prevent it
sticking to the pan.

Variation: Use beef – shin or chuck

steak – instead of mutton. If mutton
is not available use best end of neck
lamb cutlets, boned.

Liver pâté

Serves 8

8 oz	200 g	pigs liver
4 oz	100 g	pork fat
4	4	anchovy fillets
1	1	small apple
1	1	small onion
1	1	clove of garlic
1 oz	25 g	butter
2 Tbs	2 Tbs	plain flour
$\frac{1}{4}$ pt	125ml	milk
1	1	egg
1	1	bay leaf

1$\frac{1}{4}$ pint (625 ml) ovenproof dish
Preparation time about 15 min
Cooking time 1$\frac{1}{2}$ hours 325°F (160°C)
Wash the liver in cold water, dry well
and mince three times.
Peel the apple, onion and garlic.
Mince with the pork fat and anchovy
fillets, add to the liver and mix well.
Melt the butter in a small pan, add the
flour, mix well and cook for 2 - 3
minutes. Remove from the heat and
gradually add the milk. Bring to the
boil, stirring until thickened. Beat in
the egg.
Cool the sauce, then beat into the liver
mixture. Beat well until evenly blended.
Pour into the ovenproof dish. Place
the bay leaf on top and cover the dish
with greased foil.
Bake in the centre of the oven for
1$\frac{1}{2}$ hours.
Remove the foil and place a plate on
the pâté with a weight on top. Leave
until cold.
Cover with clarified butter (see tip)
and leave until set.
Serve from the dish with toast.

Tip: To clarify butter, heat gently in a

shallow wide pan. Pour off the oil,
leaving the whitish deposits behind.

Mixed grill

Serves 4

4	4	lamb chops
4	4	pork sausages
4	4	lambs kidneys
4	4	slices calves liver
4	4	tomatoes
4	4	large flat mushrooms
4	4	rashers streaky bacon
1 Tbs	1 Tbs	oil
1	1	
bunch	bunch	watercress

Preparation time about 20 min
Cooking time 18-19 min
Wipe the chops and trim off excess fat ;
prick the sausages. Remove the fat
from the kidneys and cut them in half,
remove the cores and wash them well
in cold salted water.
Wipe the liver ; halve the tomatoes ;
wash the mushrooms and derind the
bacon.
Place the chops and sausages on the
grill rack ; season well with salt and
pepper.
Put the remaining ingredients, except
the bacon, in the grill pan, season well
with salt and pepper ; brush with oil.
Put the grill pan under maximum heat
for 3-4 minutes. Put the grill rack in
position over the pan and brush the
chops and sausages with oil. Cook for
10 minutes, turning the chops and
sausages once or twice during
cooking.
Add the bacon to the rack and cook
for 5 minutes, turning once.
Wash the watercress and remove
excess stalks.
Arrange the foods on a large serving
dish and garnish with watercress.
Serve with crisps.

Baked ham slice

Serves 4

1 lb	400 g	piece middle cut gammon
2 tsp	2 tsp	soft brown sugar
6	6	cloves
2	2	cooking apples

Preparation time about 10 min
Cooking time 1¼ hours 400°F (200°C)
Soak the ham in cold water for 1 hour.
Dry well and place in a roasting tin,
sprinkle with sugar and cloves.
Peel and core the apples, slice thickly
and arrange over the ham.
Add enough water to come half way
up the sides of the ham.
Cover the tin with greased foil and
bake for 1¼ hours.
Serve with broccoli.

Variation : Use 2 onions and 4
tomatoes, sliced thickly,in place of the
sugar, cloves and cooking apples.

Braised sweetbreads

Serves 3-4

1 lb	400 g	veal sweetbreads
2 oz	50 g	butter
1	1	carrot
1	1	onion
1	1	very small turnip
1	1	stick celery
1	1	bouquet garni
1	1	clove
2 tsp	2 tsp	tomato purée
½ pint	250 ml	chicken stock
1 Tbs	1 Tbs	white wine or cider
4	4	slices fried bread
1 Tbs	1 Tbs	plain flour
1 Tbs	1 Tbs	chopped parsley

Preparation time about 20 min
Cooking time 50 min

Blanch the sweetbreads (see tip) and cool.
Melt the butter in a large stewpot.
Scrape and slice the carrot; peel and slice the onion; peel and dice the turnip; scrub and chop the celery. Add these vegetables to the butter with the bouquet garni. Toss well so that each piece is completely coated.
Add the clove.
Blend the tomato purée, stock, and wine or cider together.
Place the sweetbreads on the vegetables, add the liquid and season well with salt and pepper.
Cover the pan with a tight fitting lid and simmer gently for 45 minutes.
Melt the remaining butter in a small pan, add the flour, mix well and cook for 2-3 minutes. Remove the pan from the heat. Arrange the fried bread on a hot serving dish and place the sweetbreads on top. Keep hot.
Gradually add the liquid to the flour and butter. Bring to the boil, stirring until slightly thickened. Cook for 2-3 minutes.
Pour the sauce over the sweetbreads and sprinkle with chopped parsley.

Tip: To blanch sweetbreads, soak them in cold water for 2-3 hours. Drain. Put into a pan, cover with cold water, bring to the boil and simmer for 4-5 minutes. Drain. Place between two plates and press until firm.

Beef olives

Serves 4

4	4	thin slices topside
2	2	rashers streaky bacon
Stuffing		
2 oz	50 g	fresh white breadcrumbs
½ tsp	½ tsp	powdered thyme
½ tsp	½ tsp	powdered sage
1	1	egg
Sauce		
1 oz	25 g	butter or dripping
1	1	small onion
1 Tbs	1 Tbs	plain flour
2 tsp	2 tsp	tomato purée
1 pint	500 ml	water

Preparation time about 20 min
Cooking time 1 hour 40 min

Trim the meat and beat with a rolling pin to flatten. Season well with salt and pepper.
Remove the bacon rinds, flatten the rashers with the back of a knife and cut each rasher in half. Place a piece of bacon on each piece of meat.
To make the stuffing, combine all the ingredients together, adding a little water or stock to make a soft consistency.
Spread a quarter of the stuffing over each piece of meat, roll up like a parcel and tie with cotton.
To make the sauce, melt the butter or dripping and fry the olives for 10 minutes or until browned. Remove them from the pan.
Grate the onion and fry in the remaining butter for 5 minutes until transparent, add the flour, mix well, and cook for 2-3 minutes. Remove the

pan from the heat, stir in the tomato purée and gradually add the water. Bring to the boil, stirring all the time, until slightly thickened. Season well with salt and pepper.
Add the olives to the sauce, cover the pan and simmer for $1\frac{1}{2}$-$1\frac{3}{4}$ hours.
Lift the olives onto a serving dish, remove the cotton, strain the sauce and pour it around the meat.

Tip: For a professional finish, pipe a border of creamed potatoes around the edge of the dish.

Variation: Use veal fillet flattened thinly instead of beef.

Pork fillets with sour cream sauce

Serves 4

8 oz	200 g	prunes
3	3	pork fillets
2 oz	50 g	melted butter or pork dripping
$\frac{1}{4}$ pint	125 ml	soured cream
a pinch of		cayenne pepper

Preparation time about 30 min plus overnight soaking
Cooking time 55 min 375°F (190°C)
Soak the prunes in cold water overnight. Next day, drain them and remove the stones.
Wipe the meat and season well with salt and pepper. Make small slits in the meat and insert half the prunes. Tie with cotton to prevent them falling out during cooking.
Place the meat in a roasting tin, sprinkle with more salt and pepper, and brush with the melted butter or pork dripping.
Bake in the centre of the oven for 45 minutes.
Remove the meat and cut into slanting slices, arrange on a hot serving dish and keep warm.

Cover the remaining prunes with cold water, bring to the boil and simmer for 30 minutes or until the prunes are pulpy. Rub them through a fine sieve or liquidise them.
Add the cream and pulp to the roasting tin, mix well until evenly blended. Heat through but do not boil.
Pour the sauce over the meat. Serve garnished with twists of orange.

Tip: If the sauce is too thick, thin down with stock or water, or white wine if available.

Variation: Add 2 oz (50 g) browned almonds to the sauce and sprinkle the meat with the juice from 1 orange.

Lancashire hot pot

Serves 4

$1\frac{1}{2}$ lb	600 g	neck of mutton chops
2 lb	1 kg	potatoes
2	2	onions
1 pint	500 ml	water

Preparation time about 15 min
Cooking time 2-2$\frac{1}{2}$ hours 350°F (180°C)
Wipe the chops and season well with salt and pepper.
Peel and thickly slice the potatoes; peel and slice the onions.
Put a layer of potatoes, then onions in a casserole dish, add the meat and cover with another layer of onions, and finally potatoes.
Cover with a tight fitting lid and cook in the centre of the oven for 2-2$\frac{1}{2}$ hours. Remove the lid for the last 30 minutes to brown the potatoes.

Braised breast of lamb with tomatoes

Serves 4

2	2	breasts of lamb, boned
2	2	onions
1 Tbs	1 Tbs	chopped parsley
1	1	orange
8 oz	200 g	sausagemeat
2 Tbs	2 Tbs	oil
1 lb	400 g	carrots
14 oz	396 g	can tomatoes
1	1	red pepper (optional)

Preparation time about 15 min
Cooking time 2¼ hours 350°F (180°C)
Wipe the meat and season well with salt and pepper.
Peel and slice the onions, add half with the parsley and the orange rind to the sausagemeat, mix well and season with salt and pepper.
Spread the mixture over the lamb, roll each up and tie firmly with string.
Heat the oil and fry the lamb for 10 minutes or until beginning to brown. Remove from the pan.
Scrub the carrots and quarter if they are large, otherwise leave them whole. Core and thinly slice the pepper if used.
Fry the carrots, the rest of the onion, and the pepper in the remaining oil for 5 minutes.
Put them into a large casserole dish with the tomatoes and their juice. Place the meat on top. Season well with salt and pepper.
Cover the dish with a tight fitting lid and cook in the centre of the oven for 2 hours.

Tip: Use *Forcemeat* (see page 36) instead of the stuffing recipe.

Marinated grill

Serves 4

2	2	shallots
1 tsp	1 tsp	chopped chives
1 tsp	1 tsp	chopped parsley
1	1	clove of garlic
1 tsp	1 tsp	salt
½ tsp	½ tsp	black pepper
2 Tbs	2 Tbs	dry sherry
1 Tbs	1 Tbs	olive oil
1 Tbs	400 g	grilling steak

4 barbecue skewers
Preparation time about 15 min,
excluding marinating time
Cooking time 15 min
Peel and grate shallots, put into a shallow dish with the chives and parsley.
Peel and crush the garlic, add to the shallots with the salt, pepper, sherry and oil. Mix well until evenly blended.
Wipe the steak and cut into small cubes. Add to the marinade, toss to cover each piece. Cover the dish and leave for at least 1 hour.
Thread the meat loosely onto skewers and grill at maximum heat for 5 minutes, turning once. Reduce the heat to medium and grill for another 10 minutes.
Serve with plain boiled rice and green salad.

Tip: A garlic press is one of the few really useful gadgets available, but if you do not have one, peel the garlic and, using a heavy flat knife, flatten the clove on a board under the heel of the knife.

right Beef olives
below Pork fillets with sour
cream sauce,
Marinated grill, and
Braised breast of lamb
with tomatoes

Shepherds' pie

Serves 4

1	1	onion
1 oz	25 g	butter
2 tsp	2 tsp	plain flour
1 lb	400 g	minced, cooked beef
1 tsp	1 tsp	tomato purée
3 Tbs	3 Tbs	stock or water
1 lb	400 g	cooked, mashed potato

Preparation time about 20 min
Cooking time 30 min 375°F (190°C)
Peel and finely chop the onion.
Melt the butter and fry the onion for 5 minutes until transparent, add the flour and mix well, cook for 2-3 minutes. Remove the pan from the heat and stir in the meat, tomato purée and the water. Season well with salt and pepper.
Put the mixture into a greased 1½ pint (1 litre) pie dish and cover with potato. Fork into a pattern on top.
Bake in the centre of the oven for 30 minutes.

Tip: Use instant powdered potato if cooked potato is not available.

Variation: Use any kind of minced cooked meat or canned corned beef.

Turkish mutton

Serves 4

2 Tbs	2 Tbs	milk
1 Tbs	1 Tbs	oil
½ Tsp	½ Tsp	salt
1 lb	400 g	mutton or lamb
12	12	very small tomatoes
12	12	spring onions
4	4	bay leaves

Preparation time about 10 min,
excluding marinating time
Cooking time 15 min
Mix the milk, oil and salt together in a shallow dish.
Wipe the meat and cut into small cubes. Add to the milk and oil, cover the dish and leave for at least 2 hours. Turn the meat often.
Wash and halve the tomatoes ; peel the onions and trim ; halve the bay leaves.
Thread the meat, tomatoes, onions and bay leaf pieces on to skewers.
Grill under maximum heat for 15 minutes.
Serve with fresh undressed lettuce and plain yoghurt.

Irish stew

Serves 4

2 lb	1 kg	Middle neck lamb chops
8 oz	200 g	onions
3 lb	1½ kg	potatoes

Preparation time about 10 min
Cooking time 2½ hours
Wipe the meat and season well with salt and pepper. Put into a large stewpot.
Peel and thickly slice the onions ; cover the meat with them.
Season with salt and pepper, and cover with cold water.
Bring to the boil, cover the pan with a tight fitting lid and simmer for 1 hour.
Peel the potatoes, leave whole if small, otherwise cut them in half and add to the stewpot. Add more salt if necessary and cook for a further 1½ hours.
Arrange the potatoes around the edge of a hot serving dish and pile the lamb and onions in the centre.

Tip: If the lamb is very fatty, strain off the stock after 1 hour's cooking. Skim off the fat using kitchen paper. Return to the stewpot with the potatoes.

Poultry and Game

The cooking times and temperatures given with these recipes are intended only as a guide. Experience will show whether your tastes require slight adjustments to the length of time or degree of heat required.

Roasting times chart
Poultry

All frozen poultry and game must be completely defrosted and allowed to reach room temperature before cooking.

400°F (200°C) has been proven the temperature best suited to cook all poultry except turkeys, which because of their comparatively large size need longer, slower cooking (see chart below).

Chicken (oven ready weight) at 400°F (200°C)
3-4 lbs — 15 min per lb plus 15 min over
4-5 lbs — 12 min per lb plus 12 min over

Duck (oven ready weight) at 400°F (200°C)
4 lbs — 20 min per lb plus 20 min over
5-6 lbs — 15 min per lb plus 15 min over

Goose (oven ready weight) at 400°F (200°C)
6-8 lbs — 25 min per lb plus 25 min over
9-10 lbs — 20 min per lb plus 20 min over

Turkey (oven ready weight)

8-10 lbs	350°F (180°C)	$4\frac{1}{2}$-5 hrs
12-16 lbs	325°F (160°C)	$5\frac{1}{2}$-$6\frac{1}{2}$ hrs
over 16 lbs	300°F (150°C)	6-7 hrs
over 20 lbs	300°F (150°C)	7-8 hrs

Roasting time chart
Game

Grouse at 375°F (190°C)
15-30 min per lb depending on personal taste
Partridge at 375°F (190°C)
15-20 min
Pheasant at 375°F (190°C) 40 min

Accompaniments to poultry
Thin gravy
Make as for beef gravy (see page 17),
but use giblet stock instead of water.
To make giblet stock, put the giblets
into a pan with an onion, carrot, clove
and bouquet garni.
Bring to the boil, skim, cover the pan,
and simmer for 1 hour.
Strain, season well, and use.
Thick gravy
Make as for beef gravy (see page 17),
but use giblet stock (see above)
instead of water.
Season well.
Bread sauce
Put $\frac{1}{2}$ pint (250 ml) milk into a pan
with 1 peeled onion, 1 clove and 1 bay
leaf.
Bring to the boil, remove from the heat
and leave for 10 minutes.
Strain the milk over 2 oz fresh white
breadcrumbs.
Season well with salt and pepper, beat
until smooth.
Stir in 1 Tbs cream and 1 oz (25g)
butter just before use.
Bacon rolls
Derind streaky bacon and cut each
rasher in half.
Roll them up and thread on to skewers.
Add to the roasting pan 30 minutes
before the end of cooking time.
Sausages
Twist chipolata sausages in half and
separate.
Add to the roasting pan 30 minutes
before the end of cooking time.
Game chips
Using a sharp knife or potato peeler,
slice peeled potatoes thinly. Dry well
on a clean cloth.
Deep fry for 2-3 minutes until golden
brown.
Drain on kitchen paper and serve.

opposite top Coq au vin
opposite bottom Duck with
orange sauce, and
Turkey pasties
below Chicken Maryland

Hare casserole

Serves 4

1	1	hare
3 oz	75 g	butter
3	3	rashers streaky bacon
12	12	shallots
6	6	cloves
1 tsp	1 tsp	mixed herbs
2 pints	1 litre	
	125 ml	stock
1 oz	25 g	plain flour
¾ pint	375 ml	port wine
2 Tbs	2 Tbs	redcurrant jelly

Preparation time about 30 min
Cooking time 2 hours 350°F (180°C).
Have the hare skinned and jointed.
Fry in butter for 10 minutes or until beginning to brown. Remove from the pan and put into a large casserole dish.
Derind the bacon and cut into small pieces, brown in the remaining butter for 2-3 minutes, remove to the hare.
Peel the shallots and stick some of them with cloves. Add to the hare with the herbs and stock.
Cover the dish and cook in the centre of the oven for 2 hours.
Mix the flour with the remaining butter, add a little at a time to the casserole, stir well and add the port and redcurrant jelly.
Cook for a further 30 minutes.
Serve with rice.

Cock a leekie

Serves 6

7 lb	3½ Kg	boiling fowl, cleaned
3	3	leeks
3 oz	75 g	softened prunes (optional)

Preparation time about 10 min
Cooking time 4 hours
Wash the fowl and put it into a large saucepan. Cover with cold water,
season well with salt and pepper.
Bring to the boil, skim off the scum, and cover the pan with a tight fitting lid.
Simmer gently for 4 hours.
Wash the leeks and cut into 2 in (5 cm) lengths. Add to the pan with the prunes, if used, for the last 1 hour of cooking.
Use some of the chicken and leeks for a main meal one day and serve the left-overs in the liquid, as soup, on another occasion.

Tip: If the fowl is a particularly fatty one either leave the liquid to become quite cold after cooking, and then skim off the solid fat from the top, or add 2 oz (50 g) long grain rice to the pan for the last 15 minutes of the cooking to absorb some of the fat.

Duck with orange sauce

Serves 2-3

4-5 lb	2-2½ Kg	duck
3	3	oranges
2	2	onions
1	1	bay leaf
1	1	sprig parsley
1 Tbs	1 Tbs	cornflour
Garnish		
1	1	bunch watercress

Preparation time about 30 min
Cooking time 1½ hours 400°F (200°C)
Wash the duck, removing the giblets, and season well with salt and pepper.
Put the giblets into a pan with 1 pint (500 ml) water, salt and pepper to taste, and one of the onions, peeled.
Simmer for 1 hour.
Chop one orange roughly and put inside the duck with the second onion, cut roughly, and the bay leaf.
Place the duck on a small rack in a roasting tin and cook for 1½ hours.
Thinly peel the other two oranges and put the peel into a pan with ½ pint

(250 ml) water. Bring to the boil, remove from the heat and allow to stand for 20 minutes. Strain off the liquid and shred half the peel finely. Discard the rest.

Mix the cornflour to a smooth paste with a little of the fat from the roasting tin, add the orange liquid, made up to 1½ pints (750 ml) with strained giblet stock, and the shredded peel. Bring to the boil, stirring until thickened. Cook for 3-4 minutes.

Remove the orange, onion and bay leaf from the duck and place the bird on a large serving dish.

Garnish with watercress and sliced oranges, and serve the sauce separately.

Turkey pie

Serves 4

13 oz	315 g	packet frozen puff pastry
12 oz	300 g	cooked turkey
4 oz	100 g	sausagemeat or stuffing
4	4	rashers streaky bacon
4	4	tomatoes
1	1	egg

Preparation time about 20 min
Cooking time 40 min 425°F (220°C)
then 375°F (190°C)

Roll out the pastry to an oblong 16 in by 8 in (40 cm by 20 cm). Cut in half and press one half into a 7 in (18 cm) round pie plate.

Chop the turkey and spread over the pastry.

Shape the sausagemeat into small balls and scatter over the turkey, or if using left-over stuffing cut it into small pieces and use that.

Remove the bacon rinds and cut the rashers into small pieces. Scatter over the turkey.

Slice the tomatoes and arrange over the bacon. Season well with salt and pepper.

Moisten the edges of the pastry and cover the pie with the remaining pastry. Press the edges well together to seal.

Trim the edges, flute them with the back of a knife (see page 92) and make a small hole in the top of the pie.

Brush the pie with beaten egg and bake for 20 minutes at 425°F (220°C).

Reduce the heat to 375°F (190°C) and cook for a further 20 minutes.

Chicken Maryland

Serves 4

2 lb	1 Kg	chicken
2 Tbs	2 Tbs	plain flour
1	1	egg
2 oz	50 g	browned breadcrumbs
4	4	bananas

Deep fat for frying
Preparation time about 20 min
Cooking time 15 min

Skin and joint the chicken into four pieces, and season well with salt and pepper. Toss well in the flour.

Beat the egg with 1 Tbs water until smooth. Dip the chicken in it, then in the breadcrumbs. Do this twice.

Fry the chicken in deep fat for about 10 minutes or until cooked through. Drain on kitchen paper and keep hot.

Peel and halve the bananas. Dip in the remaining egg and breadcrumbs. Deep fry for 2-3 minutes. Drain on kitchen paper.

Arrange the chicken and bananas on a large dish.

Serve with corn and bacon or green salad.

Tip: To test the deep fat for readiness, drop a small piece of bread into the pan; if it falls to the bottom and then rises immediately the fat is hot enough.

Coq au vin

Serves 4

3 lb	1½ Kg	chicken
3 oz	75 g	butter
4 oz	100 g	mushrooms
4 oz	100 g	gammon
½	½	bottle Burgundy
2-3	2-3	cloves of garlic
1	1	bouquet garni
1 oz	25 g	plain flour
1 Tbs	1 Tbs	chopped parsley

Preparation time about 20 min
Cooking time 2 hours 10 min
300°F (150°C)

Skin and joint the chicken into 8 pieces.
Melt 2 oz (50 g) of the butter in a large
shallow pan, add the chicken and fry
for 15 minutes, turning often until
brown. Transfer to a stewpot.
Wash the mushrooms ; derind and chop
the gammon. Add both to the remaining
butter and fry for 5 minutes until the
gammon is beginning to brown.
Add to the chicken.
Heat the Burgundy in a separate pan,
set light to it and let the flames die out.
Pour over the chicken and add the
peeled garlic and the bouquet garni.
Cover with a tight fitting lid and cook
in the centre of the oven for 1½ hours.
Mix the remaining butter and the
flour together to make a paste.
Divide into small pieces and add to
the stewpot, mix well, and cook for a
further 20 minutes.
Arrange the chicken on a hot serving
dish and pour the sauce over.
Sprinkle with chopped parsley.

Tip: The Coq au vin can be cooked on
top of the cooker, over a very low heat,
for 1¼ hours, if preferred.

Turkey and ham pasties

Makes 12

2 x 13 oz	315 g	packets frozen puff pastry
4 oz	113 g	can paté de foie
8 oz	200 g	cooked turkey
4 oz	100 g	ham
2 oz	50 g	butter
1	1	small onion
1 oz	25 g	plain flour
½ pint	250 ml	milk

Preparation time about 20 min
Cooking time 17-18 min 450°F (230°C)

Roll out each packet of pastry to an
oblong 18 in by 12 in (45 cm by
30 cm) and cut out 12 6 in squares.
Spread each with a little of the paté.
Chop the turkey and ham roughly,
season well with salt and pepper.
Peel and finely chop the onion, fry for
5 minutes in the butter. Add the flour,
mix well, and cook for 2-3 minutes.
Remove the pan from the heat and
gradually add the milk.
Bring back to the boil, stirring until
thickened. Add the turkey and ham, mix
well and cool slightly.
Place a little of the mixture in the
centre of each pastry square. Moisten
the edges with water and fold in half,
pressing the edges well to seal. Brush
with milk.
Bake for 10 minutes.
Serve hot or cold.

Soups
Sauces and
Stuffings

Giblet soup

Makes 2 pints

1	1	large onion
1	1	carrot
1 oz	25 g	lard or dripping
1	1	set chicken giblets
8 oz	200 g	chuck steak
1 tsp	1 tsp	salt
½ tsp	½ tsp	black pepper
1 tsp	1 tsp	mixed herbs
1 Tbs	1 Tbs	tomato purée
2½ pints	1¼ litres	water
1 oz	25 g	butter
1 oz	25 g	plain flour

Preparation time about 25 min
Cooking time 2 hours 30 min
Peel and grate the onion ; scrub and grate the carrot.
Melt the lard or dripping and fry the onions and carrots for 10 minutes until browned. Remove from the pan.
Wash and dry the giblets and chuck steak. Cut the beef into small pieces and fry in the remaining fat for 10 minutes, turning once, until browned.
Return the vegetables to the pan with the salt, pepper and herbs.
Mix the tomato purée with the water and add to the pan.
Bring to the boil, cover the pan with a tight fitting lid, and simmer for 2 hours.
Melt the butter in another pan, add the flour, mix well and stir over a low heat for 10 minutes until the flour browns. Do not allow to burn.
Strain the stock and gradually add to the flour mixture. Bring to the boil, stirring until slightly thickened.
Remove the bones from the chicken neck, finely chop the liver and heart, discard the gizzard. Add the chopped meats and beef to the liquid. Mix well, bring back to the boil and pour into a soup tureen.

31

French onion soup

Serves 4

2 lbs	1 Kg	onions
3 oz	75 g	butter
2½ pints	1¼ litres	beef stock or water
4	4	slices French bread
1 oz	25 g	butter
3 oz	75 g	Cheddar cheese

Preparation time about 15 min
Cooking time 1 hour 10 min

Peel and thinly slice the onions. Melt the butter in a large shallow pan, add the onions and fry slowly for 30 minutes until they are evenly browned.
Add the stock or water, and salt and black pepper to taste. Bring to the boil, reduce the heat, cover the pan with a tight fitting lid and simmer for 40 minutes.
Spread the bread with butter ; grate the cheese and sprinkle thickly over the bread.
Place a slice in each of four large soup plates. Spoon the onions and liquid over and serve immediately. The heat from the liquid and onions will melt the cheese and heat it through.

Tip: Wait until the liquid has been absorbed by the bread before eating it with a soup spoon.

Tomato and celery soup

Makes 3 pints

1	1	small onion
1	1	small head celery
1 lb	400 g	tomatoes
2 oz	50 g	butter
1 tsp	1 tsp	salt
½ tsp	½ tsp	black pepper
1 tsp	1 tsp	mixed herbs
2 Tbs	2 Tbs	tomato purée
2½ pints	1¼ litres	water or stock
1 oz	25 g	plain flour
4 Tbs	4 Tbs	single cream

Preparation time about 30 min
Cooking time 2 hours

Peel and chop the onion ; scrub and chop the celery ; wash and quarter the tomatoes.
Melt the butter in a large pan, add the onions and celery and fry for 10 minutes over a low heat until the onions are transparent.
Add the tomatoes, salt, pepper and herbs. Cook for 10 minutes.
Mix the tomato purée with the water or stock, add to the pan and bring to the boil. Cover the pan and simmer for 1½ hours.
Rub the vegetables and their liquid through a fine sieve, or liquidise.
Mix the flour to a smooth paste with a little cold water. Add to the purée and bring back to the boil. Cook, stirring until thickened, for 5 minutes.
Stir in the cream, mix well and pour into a soup tureen.
Serve with toast.

Espagnole sauce

Makes 1 pint (500 ml)

2 oz	50 g	butter
2 oz	50 g	bacon
1	1	carrot
1	1	onion
4 oz	100 g	mushrooms
1 pint	500 ml	stock
3 Tbs	3 Tbs	tomato purée
2 Tbs	2 Tbs	sherry

Preparation time about 20 min
Cooking time 20 min

Melt the butter in a heavy based saucepan.
Remove the bacon rinds, add them to the pan with the bacon cut into small pieces. Fry for 10 minutes until beginning to brown.
Scrub and dice the carrot ; peel and dice the onion, add both to the pan and fry for about 10 minutes until the

onion is transparent.

Wash and slice the mushrooms, add to the pan with the other vegetables and mix well.

Add the flour, mix well and cook gently, stirring frequently for about 5 minutes until the flour is browned. Be careful at this stage not to let the flour burn.

Remove the pan from the heat and gradually add the stock, bring back to the boil, stirring until the mixture thickens slightly. Add the mushrooms, cover the pan and cook gently for 10 minutes.

Mix the tomato purée to a smooth paste with enough water to make it up to $\frac{1}{4}$ pint (125 ml). Stir into the sauce with the sherry. Cook for another 10 minutes.

Press the mixture through a fine sieve or liquidise. Reheat and use as required.

White sauce

Makes $\frac{1}{2}$ pint (250 ml)

1 oz	25 g	butter
1 oz	25 g	plain flour
$\frac{1}{2}$ pint	250 ml	milk
a pinch of		salt
a pinch of		pepper

Preparation time about 10 min
Cooking time 5 min

Melt the butter in a small pan, add the flour, mix well and cook for 2-3 minutes, stirring occasionally to prevent the mixture sticking.

Remove the pan from the heat. Gradually add the milk, stirring all the time to prevent lumps forming. Return to the heat and bring slowly to the boil, stirring all the time until thickened.

Season well with salt and pepper.

Variation 1: Caper. Add 1 tsp chopped capers and a few drops of vinegar.

2: Cheese. Add 1 oz (25 g) Parmesan or 2 oz (50 g) grated Cheddar cheese and a pinch of mustard.

3: Egg. Add 1-2 chopped hardboiled eggs.

4: Parsley. Add 1 Tbs chopped parsley.

5: Shrimp. Add 3 oz (75 g) shrimps.

Bread sauce

Makes $\frac{1}{2}$ pint (250 ml)

1	1	onion
1	1	clove
$\frac{1}{2}$ pint	250 ml	milk
1 Tbs	1 Tbs	cream
2 oz	50 g	breadcrumbs
1 oz	25 g	butter
$\frac{1}{2}$ tsp	$\frac{1}{2}$ tsp	salt
a pinch of		white pepper

Preparation time about 10 min
Cooking time 20 min

Peel the onion and put into a pan with the clove and milk. Heat very gently, leave for 15 minutes.

Remove the onion and clove, add the cream and breadcrumbs, beat until smooth.

Beat in the butter, salt and pepper.

Serve immediately.

Mint sauce

Makes enough for 1 meal

a few sprigs		mint
1 tsp	1 tsp	castor sugar
2-3 Tbs	2-3 Tbs	malt vinegar

Preparation time about 5 min plus standing time

Wash the mint leaves, dry them and chop finely with the sugar.

Put both in a small dish with a little water. Leave for 5-10 minutes.

Add the vinegar and use with lamb.

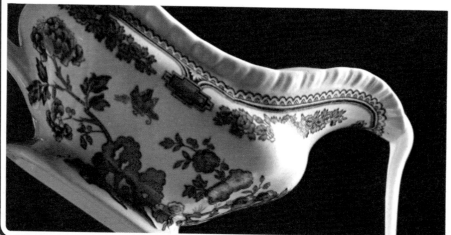

Horseradish sauce

Makes enough for 1 meal
2 oz	50 g	fresh, grated horseradish
a pinch of		castor sugar
a pinch of		dry mustard
a pinch of		salt
a pinch of		pepper
$\frac{1}{4}$ pint	125 ml	cream
1 tsp	1 tsp	wine vinegar

Preparation time about 5 min
Mix the horseradish, sugar and mustard together with salt and pepper.
Add the cream and thin down with the vinegar if necessary.
Serve with beef.

Hollandaise sauce

Makes $\frac{1}{4}$ pint (125 ml)
1 Tbs	1 Tbs	vinegar
1 Tbs	1 Tbs	water
a pinch of		salt
a pinch of		white pepper
2	2	egg yolks
3 oz	75 g	butter

Preparation time about 10 min
Put the vinegar, water, salt and pepper into a small pan. Heat to boiling and boil until the mixture is reduced by half.
Pour the liquid into a small bowl and place it over a small pan of hot water.
Add the egg yolks and whisk the mixture well.
Gradually beat in the butter a small knob at a time, whisking well after each addition.
Use immediately.

Tip: If the mixture begins to curdle, add a little cold water and whisk well.

above French onion soup
opposite top Raw ingredients for stuffings
opposite bottom White sauce

The quantities made from the stuffing recipes are suitable for small birds weighing about 3½-4 lbs.

Forcemeat stuffing

Makes about 8 oz (200 g)

1	1	rasher streaky bacon
1 oz	25 g	shredded suet
4 oz	100 g	fresh white breadcrumbs
1 tsp	1 tsp	chopped parsley
a pinch of		dried thyme
½	½	lemon
1	1	egg

Preparation time about 10 min
Derind the bacon and chop the rasher finely. Mix with the suet, breadcrumbs, parsley, thyme and the grated lemon rind.
Season well with salt and freshly ground black pepper.
Beat the egg until smooth, add to the mixture and mix well until evenly blended. Add a little stock or water if necessary to make a soft consistency.

Sage and onion stuffing

Makes about 1¼ lbs (500 g)

1 lb	400 g	onions
1 tsp	1 tsp	dried sage
4 oz	100 g	fresh white breadcrumbs
1 tsp	1 tsp	salt
½ tsp	½ tsp	black pepper
2 oz	50 g	melted butter

Preparation time about 10 min
Cooking time 20 min
Peel and halve the onions, put into a pan and cover with cold water and bring to the boil. Cover with a tight fitting lid and simmer for 15 minutes until tender. Drain and chop them finely.
Mix the onions, sage, breadcrumbs, salt and pepper together until evenly blended. Add the butter and beat well until smooth. Use to stuff goose, pork or duck.

Bacon and orange stuffing

Makes about 1 lb (400 g)

1	1	onion
4 oz	100 g	bacon pieces
4 oz	100 g	fresh white breadcrumbs
2	2	oranges
1 Tbs	1 Tbs	chopped parsley

Preparation time about 15 min
Peel and mince the onion. Fry gently in the butter for 5 minutes, until transparent.
Derind the bacon and chop finely, or mince. Fry in the remaining butter for 5 minutes.
Mix the onion, bacon and breadcrumbs together with the rind and juice from the oranges, and the parsley. Use with lamb, veal or fish.

Sausage and chestnut stuffing

Makes about 1¾ lbs (700 g)

1	1	small onion
1 oz	25 g	butter
8 oz	200 g	chestnuts
1 lb	400 g	sausagemeat
1 Tbs	1 Tbs	chopped parsley
1 tsp	1 tsp	salt
a pinch of		pepper
4 oz	100 g	fresh white breadcrumbs
1	1	lemon

Preparation time about 30 min
Peel and grate or finely chop the onion. Melt the butter and fry the onion gently for 5 minutes until transparent.
Meanwhile, put the chestnuts into a pan and cover with cold water, bring to the boil and simmer for 2-3 minutes. Drain and remove the skins.
Chop or mince the chestnuts finely, add to the onion with the sausagemeat, parsley, salt, pepper, breadcrumbs and the grated lemon rind. Beat well until evenly blended. Use with poultry.

Vegetables

Vegetables in season

January
Beetroot	Brussels sprouts
Cabbages	Carrots	Cauliflower
Celery	Jerusalem artichokes
Leeks	Parsnips	Shallots
Swedes	Turnips

Beetroot   Brussels sprouts
Cabbages   Carrots   Cauliflower
Celery   Jerusalem artichokes
Leeks   Parsnips   Shallots
Swedes   Turnips

February
Beetroot   Brussels sprouts
Cabbages   Carrots   Celeriac
Kale   Leeks   Parsnips
Swedes

March
Beetroot   Brussels sprouts
Broccoli   Cabbages   Cauliflower
Celery   Parsnips   Sea kale

April
Artichokes   Beetroot   Broccoli
Cabbages   Carrots   Chervil
Leeks   Parsnips   Sea kale
Spinach

May
Artichokes   Asparagus   Carrots
Cauliflower   Chervil   Courgettes
Peas   Potatoes *new* Spinach
Turnips

June
Artichokes   Asparagus
Beans *broad, french (kidney)*
Cabbages   Carrots   Courgettes
Leeks   Peas
Potatoes *new* Spinach   Turnips

July
Artichokes   Beans *broad, runner*
Beetroot   Cabbages   Carrots
Cauliflower   Celery   Courgettes
Leeks   Marrows   Onions
Parsnips   Peas   Potatoes
Spinach   Sweetcorn   Turnips

August
Artichokes   Beans *broad, runner*
Beetroot   Cabbages   Carrots
Cauliflower   Celery   Courgettes
Leeks   Marrows   Parsnips
Peas   Potatoes   Spinach
Sweetcorn   Turnips

September

Artichokes	Beetroot	
Brussels sprouts		Cabbages
Carrots	Celeriac	Celery
Leeks	Marrows	Onions
Parsnips	Peas	Spinach
Swedes	Turnips	

October

Beetroot	Brussels sprouts	
Cabbages	Cauliflower	Celeriac
Celery	Marrows	Onions
Parsnips	Turnips	

November

Beetroot	Brussels sprouts	
Cabbages	Carrots	Celeriac
Celery	Jerusalem artichokes	
Leeks	Marrows	Onions
Turnips		

December

Broccoli	Cabbages	Carrots
Celeriac	Celery	
Jerusalem artichokes		Leeks
Onions	Parsnips	Spinach
Brussels sprouts		Turnips

Serving suggestions

Beans (French and runner)
Toss cooked, drained beans in 1 oz (25 g) butter or oil, freshly milled black pepper, 1 small clove crushed garlic and juice from ½ lemon.

Celery
To braise celery, wash and quarter lengthwise 2 heads of celery. Fry for 5 minutes in 2 oz (50 g) butter until slightly browned. Add 1 pint (500 ml) chicken stock, cover with rashers of streaky bacon and simmer, covered, for 1 hour, or cook in the base of a moderate oven for at least 1 hour.

Corn on the cob
Remove the leaves and tassels, and rinse the cobs in cold water. Plunge them into boiling, salted water and cook for 6-8 minutes. Drain well, and serve with salt, freshly ground black pepper and plenty of melted butter.

above raw ingredients for
Tomato salad,
Leek salad, and
Sweet and sour beetroot
opposite top Baked onions
opposite bottom Corn on the cob

Carrots (Vichy)
Cook sliced carrots in a large covered pan with 2 Tbs stock, 2 oz (50 g) butter, juice of $\frac{1}{2}$ lemon, salt and pepper until they are soft. Serve sprinkled with chopped parsley.

Jerusalem artichokes
Wash well, peel artichokes and place immediately in a large bowl of cold salted water to prevent discolouration. Cook in salted boiling water for 20 minutes or until tender. Drain and serve with *White sauce* (see page 33).

Mushrooms
Wash large mushrooms and remove the stalks. Place the caps skin side down in a shallow ovenproof dish. Dot each with a little butter and cook in the centre of a moderate oven for 5 minutes.
To make stuffed mushrooms, make up a *Forcemeat* stuffing (see page 36) and divide between the mushrooms. Dot with butter and cook for a further 10 minutes.
Serve as they are or with *White sauce* (see page 33).

Duchesse Potatoes
Add 1 oz (25 g) butter and 1 egg to 1 lb cooked, sieved potatoes. Beat well and place the mixture in a forcing bag. Pipe swirls on a greased baking tin. Brush with beaten egg, and bake in the centre of a moderate oven for 10 minutes until they are browned.

Scalloped Potatoes
Slice peeled potatoes and onions thinly into a deep ovenproof dish. Season each layer well with salt and pepper.
Add milk to almost cover the potatoes and bake in the centre of a moderate oven for 1-1$\frac{1}{2}$ hours.

Tomato salad

Serves 4

1 lb	400 g	tomatoes
4 Tbs	4 Tbs	oil
1 Tbs	1 Tbs	lemon juice
1 tsp	1 tsp	soy sauce
1 tsp	1 tsp	Worcester sauce

Preparation time about 10 min, plus standing time
Put the tomatoes into a bowl and cover with boiling water. Leave for a few seconds, drain and peel off the skins.
Slice the tomatoes thinly into a shallow dish.
Put the oil, lemon juice, soy and Worcester sauces into a screwtop jar and shake vigorously until the mixture is evenly blended.
Pour over the tomatoes, sprinkle with salt and black pepper, cover and leave for 2 hours before serving.

Leek salad

Serves 4

2	2	large leeks
1	1	small cucumber
1 Tbs	1 Tbs	chopped chives
1 tsp	1 tsp	curry paste
$\frac{1}{2}$ pint	250 ml	yoghurt
a pinch of		cayenne pepper

Preparation time about 15 min
Wash the leeks thoroughly, and cut the white part into very thin slices.
Peel and slice the cucumber, mix with the leeks.
Mix the chives, curry paste and yoghurt together and pour over the leeks. Mix well, pile into a serving dish and sprinkle with cayenne pepper.

Tip: Use this salad immediately otherwise the cucumber will make the mixture wet. If you want to prepare the salad in advance, put the cucumber in a colander and sprinkle with salt. Leave for at least 30 minutes before using.

Cabbage salad

Serves 4

8 oz	200 g	white cabbage
2 oz	50 g	walnuts
4 oz	100 g	Cheshire cheese
1 oz	25 g	wheat germ
$\frac{1}{4}$ pint	125 ml	yoghurt

Preparation time about 15 min
Shred or grate the cabbage into a large bowl.
Chop the nuts and mix with the cabbage.
Grate the cheese and add to the cabbage with the wheat germ.
Season well with salt and black pepper.
Mix the yoghurt into the cabbage mixture and toss well.
Serve very cold.

Braised peas

Serves 4

6	6	button onions or shallots
1 lb	400 g	peas
1	1	lettuce
1 oz	25 g	butter
1	1	bouquet garni
a pinch of		pepper
$\frac{1}{2}$ tsp	$\frac{1}{2}$ tsp	salt
a pinch of		castor sugar
3 Tbs	3 Tbs	water or stock

Preparation time about 10 min
Cooking time 50 min 350°F (180°C)
Peel the onions ; shell the peas ; wash and shred the lettuce.
Melt the butter in a large saucepan, add the vegetables, toss well in the butter ; transfer to a casserole dish.

Add the remaining ingredients and mix well. Cover the dish with a tight fitting lid.
Cook in the centre of the oven for 50 minutes.
Remove the bouquet garni and serve.

Tip: an alternative method is to line the casserole dish with whole lettuce leaves instead of shredding them.

Thatched broad beans

Serves 4-6

2 lb	1 Kg	broad beans, shelled
1 oz	25 g	butter
1	1	small onion
1 oz	25 g	plain flour
$\frac{1}{2}$ pint	250 ml	milk
$\frac{1}{2}$	$\frac{1}{2}$	lemon
8	8	rashers streaky bacon
1 Tbs	1 Tbs	chopped parsley

Preparation time about 20 min
Cooking time 15 min
Cook the beans in a little salted, boiling water for 6-7 minutes or until tender. Drain.
Melt the butter ; peel and chop the onion, fry in the butter for 5 minutes.
Add the flour, mix well and cook for 2-3 minutes.
Remove the pan from the heat and gradually add the milk, bring back to the boil, stirring until slightly thickened.
Add the grated lemon rind and mix well. Season to taste with salt and black pepper.
Pour the sauce over the beans in a shallow dish.
Criss-cross the bacon over the top, and grill until crisp.
Serve immediately.

Tip: Use a 12 oz (341.2 g) packet frozen broad beans when fresh ones are not available.

Baked onions

Serves 4

4	4	Spanish onions
4 oz	100 g	cooked meat
1 oz	25 g	fresh white breadcrumbs
2 oz	50 g	Cheddar cheese
½ pint	250 ml	beef stock or water

Preparation time about 20 min
Cooking time 55 min
Peel the onions and boil in salted water for 10 minutes. Drain.
Remove the centres (see tip) and chop them finely ; mince the meat and mix with the onion centres.
Fill the onion shells, piling the mixture into a peak on top.
Mix the cheese and breadcrumbs together and sprinkle over the tops.
Place in an ovenproof dish and add the stock.
Bake for 45 minutes.
Serve immediately, with tomato sauce.

Tip: To remove centres hold onion wrapped in a cloth and gently squeeze out the centre. Use a spoon if necessary.

Artichokes with eggs

Serves 4

4	4	large globe artichokes
4 oz	112 g	can pâté de foie
4	4	eggs
¼ pint	125 ml	mayonnaise
a pinch of		cayenne pepper

Preparation time about 20 min
Cooking time 20 min
Wash the artichokes well in cold water.
Cook in salted, boiling water for 15 minutes. Drain and pull off the petals.
Remove the flower and leave the bottoms to cool.
Spread each bottom with pâté.
Poach the eggs for 4 minutes. Drain

and leave to cool. Place one on each layer of pâté.
Season the mayonnaise well with salt and pepper, pour over the eggs and sprinkle with cayenne pepper.
Serve on a bed of shredded lettuce.

Cauliflower au gratin

Serves 4

1	1	large cauliflower
1 pint	500 ml	cheese sauce
2 oz	50 g	Cheddar cheese
1 oz	25 g	fresh white breadcrumbs

Preparation time about 15 min
Cooking time 15 min
Break the cauliflower into flowerets. Wash well in cold water.
Cook in salted ,boiling water for 10 minutes or until tender but not soft. Drain well.
Make the cheese sauce (see page 33). **Put** cauliflower into a shallow ovenproof dish and cover with the cheese sauce.
Grate the Cheddar cheese and mix with the breadcrumbs, sprinkle over the sauce and grill for 5 minutes or until browned.

Aubergines provençale

Serves 4

2	2	large aubergines
1 Tbs	1 Tbs	salt
4	4	tomatoes
3 Tbs	3 Tbs	oil
1 oz	25 g	plain flour
1	1	clove of garlic
½ tsp	½ tsp	black pepper
½ tsp	½ tsp	salt
1 Tbs	1 Tbs	chopped parsley

Preparation time about 15 min plus standing time
Cooking time 20 min

Peel the aubergines and cut into $\frac{1}{2}$ in (2 cm) lengths. Sprinkle with the salt and leave for at least 1 hour.
Cover the tomatoes with boiling water, leave for a few seconds, drain, and remove the skins. Chop the flesh finely.
Heat 1 Tbs of the oil and cook the tomatoes gently for 5 minutes.
Drain the aubergines, dry them and toss in the flour. Fry in the remaining oil for 10 minutes, turning them until brown. Add to the tomatoes. Peel and crush the garlic, add to the tomatoes with the pepper, salt and parsley. Mix well and cook for 5 minutes.
Serve immediately.

Glazed carrots

Serves 4

1 lb	400 g	carrots
2 oz	50 g	butter
1 oz	25 g	brown sugar
1 tsp	1 tsp	lemon juice
1 Tbs	1 Tbs	chopped parsley

Preparation time about 15 min
Cooking time 30 min
Scrub the carrots and cut into rings if large, otherwise leave whole.
Cook in salted, boiling water for 10 minutes or until softened slightly.
Drain and add the butter, sugar and lemon juice.
Mix well and cook very gently over a low heat until the sugar has dissolved.
Cover the pan with a tight fitting lid and cook gently for about 20 minutes or until the carrots are tender and the sugar has caramelized over them.
Shake the pan from time to time.
Toss in chopped parsley and serve immediately.

Sweet and sour beetroot

Serves 4-6

1 lb	400 g	cooked beetroot
1 oz	25 g	butter
1 oz	25 g	soft brown sugar
$\frac{1}{2}$ oz	12 g	cornflour
$\frac{1}{4}$ pint	125 ml	malt vinegar
$\frac{1}{4}$ pint	125 ml	water

Preparation time about 15 min
Cooking time 5 min
Peel and dice the beetroot.
Melt the butter, add the sugar and heat gently until the sugar dissolves.
Mix the cornflour to a smooth paste with a little of the vinegar. Add the rest and mix with the sugar and butter. Bring to the boil, stirring until slightly thickened.
Add the beetroot to the sauce. Mix well and leave until cool.
Sprinkle with chopped parsley.
Serve hot or cold with cold meats.

Omelets Soufflés and Batters

Plain omelet

Serves 1

3	3	eggs
½ tsp	½ tsp	salt
a pinch of		black pepper
1 oz	25 g	butter

Preparation time about 10 min
Cooking time 2-3 min
Beat the eggs until smooth, season well with salt and pepper.
Melt the butter in an omelet pan and when very hot, pour in the eggs.
Shake the pan with the left hand immediately, and fork the mixture from the edges of the pan to the centre with the right hand, until the mixture is firm underneath but still wet on top.
Flip one third of the omelet over and shake it down the edge of the pan, turn it onto a hot plate, rolling it into three as it falls from the pan.
The finished omelet should be the shape of a large cigar when finished.
Serve immediately.

Variations 1: Fine herbes. Add 1 Tbs mixed, fresh chopped herbs such as parsley and chives, or chervil or thyme with basil and marjoram, to the egg mixture before adding it to the pan. Or sprinkle the herbs on top of the cooked omelet before folding it in three.
2: Bacon. Add 2 rashers of streaky bacon, derinded, chopped and lightly fried, to the egg mixture.
3: Cheese. Add 1 oz grated Cheddar cheese to the egg mixture and sprinkle the finished omelet with Parmesan cheese.
4: Ham. Add 2 oz (50 g) chopped ham to the egg mixture as it is cooking.
5: Mushroom. Add 2 oz (50 g) mushrooms cooked in the following way. Wash and dice the mushrooms, fry them in a little butter with a squeeze of lemon juice and some black pepper.

Drain and add to the cooked omelet before it is folded.

6: Orange (serves 2). Thickly peel 1 orange. Cut the flesh into small pieces and put into a pan with 1 Tbs brown sugar. Heat gently until the sugar has dissolved and the orange is hot. Add to the cooked omelet before it is folded.

French omelet

Serves 4

4	4	eggs
4 Tbs	4 Tbs	milk
1 oz	25 g	butter
2 Tbs	2 Tbs	clear honey
1 oz	25 g	walnuts

10 in (25 cm) frying pan
Preparation time about 15 min
Cooking time 4-5 min

Separate the eggs and whisk the egg yolks and milk together until slightly thickened.
Whisk the whites until stiff and standing in peaks.
Melt the butter in the pan.
Add a little of the egg whites to the egg yolk mixture, whisk until smooth. Fold the remaining egg whites into the egg yolk mixture with a metal spoon.
Pour the mixture into the pan and cook gently for 4-5 minutes until firm.
Meanwhile, heat the honey in a small pan ; chop the nuts finely and add to the honey.
Put the omelet under a hot grill for 2-3 minutes to brown.
Turn the omelet onto a warm plate, pour the honey mixture into the centre and fold the omelet in half.
Serve immediately.

Variations 1: Use apricot jam and chopped blanched almonds, instead of the honey and walnuts.
2: Use chocolate sauce and raisins.

Baked soufflé

Serves 4

1 oz	25 g	butter
1 oz	25 g	plain flour
¼ pint	125 ml	milk
1 Tbs	1 Tbs	castor sugar
a few drops of vanilla essence		
3	3	egg yolks
4	4	egg whites

6 in. (15 cm) soufflé dish
Preparation time about 20 min
Cooking time 25 min 400°F (200°C)

Prepare the soufflé dish (see page 47).
Melt the butter in a heavy based pan. Add the flour, mix well and cook for 2-3 minutes. Remove the pan from the heat.
Gradually stir in the milk, bring to the boil, stirring until the mixture is thick and leaves the sides of the pan clean.
Beat in the castor sugar and essence with the egg yolks.
Whisk the egg whites until they form soft peaks, and fold into the mixture with a metal spoon.
Spoon the mixture into the prepared dish.
Bake for 25 minutes.

Variations 1: Cheese. Omit the sugar and essence and add 4 oz (100 g) grated Cheddar cheese, a pinch of cayenne pepper and a pinch of dry mustard.
2: Fish. Omit the sugar and essence and add 4 oz (100 g) cooked flaked fish. Make the sauce with fish liquid, if available, instead of milk, and add 1 Tbs chopped parsley.
3: Chocolate. Break 2 oz (50 g) plain chocolate into a pan with the milk, heat gently to dissolve it before adding the mixture to the sauce.
4: Pineapple. Drain a 10 oz (283.5 g) can pineapple, dry well and arrange ⅔ of the slices over the base of the soufflé dish. Chop the rest finely and add to the sauce.

Soufflé omelet

Serves 4

3	3	egg yolks
1½ oz	40 g	castor sugar
4	4	egg whites
a pinch of		salt

Preparation time about 15 min
Cooking time 20 min 375°F (190°C)
Whisk the egg yolks and sugar together until thick.
Whisk the egg whites until stiff but avoid peaking.
Fold the egg whites into the egg yolk mixture using a metal spoon.
Pour the mixture into a greased 1½ pint pie dish. Make an indentation in the top with a knife.
Bake in the centre of the oven for 15-20 minutes.
Sprinkle with castor sugar and serve immediately.

What went wrong and why
Flat-Egg whites over-whisked.
Unevenly risen-Panada and egg whites too stiff.
Collapsed during cooking-Dish too small. Overcooked.

Preparing the dish
Grease a soufflé dish with butter. Measure a double thickness band of foil or greaseproof paper long enough to wrap around the outside of the dish and deep enough to stand at least 2 in. above the rim. Grease the band, wrap it around the dish, and secure with a piece of string. Prepare small dishes in the same way, but stand them on a baking tin for easy removal from the oven after cooking.

opposite top Fruit fritters
opposite bottom Plain omelet
below Chocolate soufflé

Basic pouring batter

Makes ¾ pint (375 ml)
4 oz　　100 g　plain flour
a pinch of　　salt
1　　1　　egg
½ pint　250 ml milk

Preparation time about 10 min
Sift the flour and salt into a bowl,
make a well in the centre and add the
egg and a little of the milk.
Beat the mixture to a smooth paste,
then gradually add the rest of the milk,
beating well with a wooden spoon
until the surface is covered with small
bubbles.
Use as required.

Variations 1: Yorkshire pudding. Heat
1 oz (25 g) lard or dripping in a shallow
roasting pan in the top of the oven.
Pour in the batter and cook at 425°F
(220°C) for 30 minutes.
2: Toad in the hole. Proceed as for
Yorkshire pudding, but add 1 lb (400 g)
sausages to the batter immediately.
Cook for 40 minutes.
3: Pancakes. Have ready a jug of
melted lard, a palette knife and 10
squares of foil or greaseproof paper.
Pour a little of the lard into an 8 in.
(20 cm) pan, tilting the pan so that the
lard covers the base completely. Heat
until smoking, and pour off excess.
Pour a little batter into the pan, tilting
it to ensure an even spread, and cook
for 2-3 minutes until the pancake is
golden brown. Turn or toss the pancake
and cook for 1-2 minutes on the other
side. Flip on to a square of foil and
cover with another square. Make 7-8
more pancakes in the same way.
Pancakes layered like this, then
wrapped in more foil, will keep fresh
and ready for use for up to 10 days if
stored in the refrigerator.

Basic fritter batter 1

Makes ½ pint (250 ml)
4 oz　　100 g　plain flour
a pinch of　　salt
1　　1　　egg
1 pint　250 ml milk

Preparation time about 5 min
Sift the flour and salt into a bowl.
Separate the egg, and add the yolk
and half the milk to the flour. Beat well
with a wooden spoon until smooth,
then beat in the rest of the milk.
Whisk the egg white until stiff and
fold into the batter just before using.

Banana sandwich fritters
Make thin banana sandwiches, cut
into fingers. Dip in batter and fry for
1-2 minutes in deep, hot fat until
golden brown. Drain on kitchen paper
and sprinkle with castor sugar to serve.

Basic fritter batter 2

Makes ½ pint (250 ml)
4 oz　　100 g　plain flour
a pinch of　　salt
1 Tbs　1 Tbs　oil
7 Tbs　7 Tbs　water
1　　1　　egg white

Preparation time about 5 min
Sift the flour and salt into a bowl. Add
the oil and water and beat to a smooth
paste with a wooden spoon.
Whisk the egg white until stiff and
fold into the batter just before using.

Fruit Fritters
Drain a 10 oz (283.5 g) can pineapple
slices. Dry them well on kitchen paper.
Dip in the batter and fry in deep, hot
fat for 3-4 minutes until golden brown
and crisp. Drain on kitchen paper and
sprinkle with brown sugar and finely
chopped walnuts.

Pastry

The cooking times and temperatures given with these recipes are intended only as a guide. Experience will show whether your tastes require slight adjustments to the length of time or degree of heat required.

Bacon and egg pie

Serves 4

8 oz	200 g	shortcrust pastry
8 oz	200 g	smoked streaky bacon
4	4	eggs
1 Tbs	1 Tbs	chopped chives
a pinch of		black pepper

7 in (17 cm) pie plate
Preparation time about 20 min
excluding pastry making
Cooking time 35 min 425°F (220°C)
then 350°F (180°C)
Make the pastry (see method page 92).
Roll it out to an oblong 16 in by 8 in (40 cm by 20 cm). Cut in half to make two 8 in (20 cm) squares and line the pie plate with one piece.
Derind the bacon, chop finely and sprinkle half over the pastry.
Break the eggs on top of the bacon, sprinkle with a little salt, the black pepper, chives and the remaining bacon.
Brush the edge of the pastry with water, and cover with the other piece of pastry, pressing the edge together to seal.
Trim, knock back and flute the edges (see page 92). Make a hole in the top and decorate with pastry trimming shaped into leaves.
Brush the top of the pie with milk and bake at the higher temperature for 15 minutes. Reduce the temperature and cook for a further 20 minutes.
Serve hot or cold with salad.

Variation: Sandwich 3 tomatoes, sliced and seasoned with salt, between 8 oz (200 g) sausagemeat, halved and rolled out to fit the plate.

Yorkshire cheesecake

6 oz	150 g	flan pastry
2	2	eggs
1 oz	25 g	castor sugar
½ pint	250 ml	curd cheese
4 Tbs	4 Tbs	evaporated milk
1	1	lemon

a few drops of almond essence

7 in (17 cm) flan ring on a baking tin
Preparation time about 25 min
excluding pastry making.
Cooking time 45 min 425°F (220°C)
then 375°F (190°C)
Make the pastry (see method page 93).
Roll it out and line the flan ring (see
page 93). Trim the edges and bake
'blind' at the higher temperature for
20 minutes.
Beat the eggs and sugar together until
smooth, add the curd and evaporated
milk with the rind and juice of the lemon
and the essence. Beat well until smooth.
Pour into the flan case and bake at the
lower temperature for 25 minutes.

Variation: Sprinkle 3 oz (75 g)
sultanas over the pastry before adding
the curd mixture.

Sausage rolls

Makes 8-12

8 oz	200 g	flaky pastry
12 oz	300 g	sausage meat
1	1	egg

Preparation time about 20 min
excluding pastry making.
Cooking time 20 min 425°F (220°C)
Make the pastry (see method page 94).
Roll it out and follow the method
shown on page 95.
Place the rolls on a wetted baking tin.
Beat the egg with a little water and
brush each roll with it.
Bake for 20 minutes. Serve hot or cold.

opposite top Mince pies
opposite bottom Sausage rolls, and
Beefsteak and kidney pie
below Vol au vent

Mince pies

Makes 12

8 oz	200 g	shortcrust pastry
3 Tbs	3 Tbs	mincemeat
1	1	egg white
1 oz	25 g	castor sugar

*Preparation time about 20 min
excluding pastry making
Cooking time 25 min 425°F (220°C)*
Make the pastry (see method page 92).
Roll it out thinly and cut out 12 rounds
using a 2½ in (6 cm) cutter and 12
rounds using a 2 in (4 cm) cutter.
Line 12 patty tins with the larger rounds.
Put a little of the mincemeat in each
of the lined tins.
Beat the egg white until smooth, brush
the edges of the pastry with egg white
and press the smaller rounds into
position.
Brush the tops with egg white and
sprinkle with the castor sugar.
Bake for 25 minutes.

Quiche lorraine

Serves 4

4 oz	100 g	shortcrust pastry
3 oz	75 g	ham
2	2	eggs
¼ pint	125 ml	milk
¼ pint	125 ml	cream
a pinch of		cayenne pepper

*6 in (15 cm) flan ring on baking tin
Preparation time about 15 min
excluding pastry making
Cooking time 30 min 425°F
(220°C) then 350°F (180°C)*
Make the pastry (see method page 92).
Roll it out thinly to fit the flan ring
(see page 93).
Chop the ham finely and fry gently in
the butter for 5 minutes. Drain.
Beat the eggs until smooth, mix with
the milk and cream. Add the ham,

cayenne pepper and salt to taste.
Pour into the prepared flan ring and
bake for 15 minutes at the higher
temperature. Reduce the heat and
cook for a further 15 minutes.

Chicken pie

*Serves 4
Filling*

3	3	chicken joints
1	1	onion
1	1	carrot
1	1	bouquet garni
6	6	peppercorns
1 tsp	1 tsp	salt
2 Tbs	2 Tbs	dry vermouth or cider
4 oz	4 oz	mushrooms
Sauce		
1 oz	25 g	butter
1 oz	25 g	plain flour
8 oz	200 g	shortcrust pastry

*2 pint (1 litre) pie dish
Preparation time about 30 min
excluding pastry making
Cooking time 1½ hours 350°F (180°C)
then 425°F (220°C)*
Wipe the chicken and season well
with salt and pepper.
Peel and slice the onion; scrub and
slice the carrot.
Put the chicken and vegetables in the
dish with the bouquet garni,
peppercorns and salt.
Add the vermouth or cider, and enough
water to cover.
Cover the dish with a tight fitting lid
or a piece of greased foil.
Bake in the centre of the oven at the
lower temperature for 1 hour.
Remove the chicken bones and return
the meat to the pie dish.
Melt the butter in a small pan, add the
flour and mix well, cook for 2-3
minutes. Remove from the heat and
gradually add ½ pint of the chicken

liquid, bring to the boil, stirring until the sauce thickens. Pour over the chicken. Cool.
Make the pastry (see method page 92).
Roll it out to fit the top of the pie dish. and cover (see page 92).
Make a hole in the top and decorate with pastry leaves.
Bake at the higher temperature for 30 minutes. Cover the top of the pie for the last 10 minutes.
Serve hot or cold.

Variation: Use turkey or beef instead of chicken ; cook the beef for 1½ hours in the oven before adding the pastry.

Cheese d'artois

Makes 24

8 oz	200 g	flaky pastry
1	1	egg
4 oz	100 g	Cheddar cheese
a pinch of		cayenne pepper
a pinch of		mustard powder

Preparation time about 20 min excluding pastry making
Cooking time 10 min 425°F (220°C)
Make the pastry (see method page 94).
Roll it out to an oblong 12 in by 8 in (30 cm by 20 cm).
Cut in half to make two pieces 6 in by 8 in (15 cm by 20 cm).
Separate the egg and beat the white until smooth. Grate the cheese and add to the egg white with the cayenne and mustard. Mix well.
Spread the mixture evenly over one square of pastry to within ½ in (1 cm) of the edge.
Brush the edge with egg yolk and place the other piece of pastry on top, pressing the edge together to seal. Beat the egg yolk with a little water and brush over the top of the pastry.
Cut into thin fingers 2 in long by ½ in wide. Twist from the centre to make

them look like bows (see page 95).
Place on wetted baking tins and bake for 10 minutes. Reverse the trays after 5 minutes.
Serve warm.

Russian fish pie

Serves 4

8 oz	200 g	white fish
1	1	hard boiled egg
1 Tbs	1 Tbs	chopped parsley
½	½	lemon
1 oz	25 g	butter
1 oz	25 g	plain flour
¼ pint	125 ml	milk
½ tsp	½ tsp	salt
a pinch of		pepper
1	1	egg
12 oz	300 g	flaky pastry

Preparation time about 20 min excluding pastry making
Cooking time 40 min 425°F (220°C) then 350°F (180°C)
Wash and dry the fish. Chop and remove the bones and skin.
Chop the hard boiled egg and mix with the fish, parsley and lemon juice.
Melt the butter, add the flour, mix well and cook for 2-3 minutes.
Remove from the heat and gradually add the milk, bring to the boil, stirring until thick. Add to the fish and mix well.
Season well with salt and pepper.
Separate the egg and add the yolk to the fish mixture. Mix well.
Make the pastry (see method page 94).
Roll it out to a 12 in (30 cm) square.
Beat the egg white and brush the edges of the pastry with it.
Place the fish mixture in the centre of the pastry square. Fold up as shown on page 94.
Bake at the higher temperature for 15 minutes. Lower the temperature and cook for a further 25 minutes.
Serve hot or cold.

left Palmiers,
Eccles cakes, and
Cream horns
below Savoury eclairs

Cream horns

Makes 16

8 oz	200 g	flaky pastry
1 Tbs	1 Tbs	seedless jam
$\frac{1}{4}$ pint	125 ml	double cream

Metal horn tins
Preparation time about 25 min
excluding pastry making
Cooking time 10 min 425°F (220°C)

Make the pastry (see method page 94).
Roll it out thinly to a square and follow the method shown on page 94.
Brush with beaten egg and place them on wetted baking tins.
Bake for 10 minutes. Reverse the trays after 5 minutes.
Remove immediately from the tins and cool on a wire rack.
Fill the ends with jam.
Whip the cream and pipe or spoon into the horns.

Beefsteak and kidney pie

Serves 4

1 lb	400 g	beef steak
2	2	lamb's kidneys
1 oz	25 g	plain flour
1 tsp	1 tsp	salt
$\frac{1}{2}$ tsp	$\frac{1}{2}$ tsp	pepper
$\frac{1}{4}$ pint	125 ml	stock or water
8 oz	200 g	flaky pastry

$1\frac{1}{4}$ pint (625 ml) pie dish
Preparation time about 30 min
excluding pastry making
Cooking time 2 hours 300°F (150°C)
then 425°F (220°C)

Wipe the meat and trim off excess fat and gristle. Cut the flesh into small pieces.
Remove the kidney fat, cut them in half and remove the cores. Cut each kidney half in 4.
Mix the flour, salt and pepper together, toss the beef and kidney in it and place in the pie dish. Cover with stock.
Cover the dish with foil and bake in the centre of the oven for $1\frac{1}{2}$ hours. Cool.
Make the pastry (see method page 94).
Roll it out and cover the pie (see page 92).
Bake at the higher temperature for 30 minutes.

Eccles cakes

Makes 8

8 oz	200 g	flaky pastry
Filling		
1 oz	25 g	butter
3 oz	75 g	currants
3 oz	75 g	chopped mixed peel
1 oz	25 g	castor sugar
1 oz	25 g	soft brown sugar
Glaze		
1	1	egg white
1 Tbs	1 Tbs	castor sugar

Preparation time about 25 min
excluding pastry making
Cooking time 20 min 425°F (220°C)

Make the pastry (see method page 94).
Roll it out to $\frac{1}{8}$ in thick and cut into eight 3 in rounds.
Melt the butter, add the currants, peel and sugars, mix well.
Follow the method shown on page 95.
Bake for 20 minutes. Reverse the trays after 15 minutes.

Vol au vent

½ lb	200 g	puff pastry
1	1	egg
Filling		
1 oz	25 g	butter
1 oz	25 g	plain flour
½ pint	250 ml	milk
8 oz	200 g	white fish
2 oz	50 g	peeled prawns
1 Tbs	1 Tbs	chopped parsley
1 Tbs	1 Tbs	chopped chives
1	1	lemon

Preparation time about 30 min
excluding pastry making
Cooking time 30 min 450°F (230°C)
then 400°F (200°C)
Make the pastry (see method page 96).
Beat the egg.
Roll out the pastry to an 8 in (20 cm)
square, and make a vol au vent case as
shown on page 96.
Place on a wetted baking tin and brush
the top with the beaten egg.
Bake at the higher temperature for
10 minutes and then at the
lower temperature for another 20
minutes.
Meanwhile make the sauce. Melt the
butter, add the flour, mix well and
cook for 2-3 minutes.
Put the milk into another pan with
the fish, salt and pepper. Bring to the
boil ; lift out the fish, flake and remove
the bones.
Gradually add the milk to the butter
and flour mixture, stirring all the time.
Bring to the boil and stir until
thickened.
Add the fish, prawns, parsley, chives
and the grated rind of the lemon.
Mix well.
Remove the centre of the vol au vent
case carefully, and cut away any damp
pastry.
Fill with the fish mixture and put the
lid in position.
Serve warm.

Vanilla slices

Makes 15

8 oz	200 g	puff pastry
Filling		
8 oz	200 g	seedless raspberry jam
¼ pint	125 ml	double cream
Icing		
4 oz	100 g	icing sugar
½	½	lemon

Preparation time about 25 min
excluding pastry making
Cooking time 15 min 425°F (220°C)
Make the pastry (see method page 96).
Roll it out to a 12 in square. Cut out
three strips each 4 in wide.
Place them on wetted baking tins
and bake for 15 minutes. Reverse the
trays after 10 minutes.
Cool on a wire rack, then slit in half
lengthwise.
Heat the jam slightly and spread over
the bases of the three slices. Whip the
cream until thick and spread over the
jam.
Sandwich the layers together in
pairs.
Sift the icing sugar into a small bowl,
add the juice from the ½ lemon, and
enough hot water to make a soft icing.
Spread it over the top of the slices.
Mark each into five and cut through
when the icing has set.

Palmiers

Makes 24

8 oz	200 g	puff pastry
Filling		
1	1	egg white
1 oz	25 g	castor sugar

Preparation time about 15 min
excluding pastry making.
Cooking time 10 min 425°F (220°C)
Make the pastry (see method page 96).
Roll it out thinly. Trim the edges

straight and brush surface with beaten
egg white.
Loosely roll the sides to the centre,
brush with more egg white and fold
one side on top of the other side.
Cut the rolled pastry into $\frac{1}{2}$ in strips,
as shown on page 96.
Bake for 10 minutes. Reverse the
trays after 5 minutes.
Cool on a wire rack.

Eclairs

Makes 14
$2\frac{1}{2}$ oz   65 g   quantity choux paste
Filling
$\frac{1}{2}$ pint   250 ml double cream
1 oz   25 g   castor sugar
Topping
6 oz   150 g   plain chocolate

*Preparation time about 30 min
excluding pastry making
Cooking time 30 min 425°F (220°C)
then 350°F (180°C)*
Make the choux paste (see method
page 97).
Put it into a forcing bag and pipe 14
3 inch lengths on to greased baking
sheets as shown on page 97.
Bake at the higher temperature for
20 minutes. Reverse the trays, reduce
the heat and cook for a further 10
minutes.
Cool on a wire rack, split each eclair
and remove the damp paste from the
centre.
Whip the cream and sugar together
until stiff. Fill the eclairs.
Break the chocolate into a small basin
and place it over a pan of hot water
until the chocolate melts.
Spread the chocolate evenly over the
top of each eclair and allow to harden
before serving.

Variation: Savoury eclairs. Beat 2 oz
(50 g) grated cheese, 2 oz (50 g)

chopped ham, 1 Tbs tomato sauce
and 1 finely grated shallot together, and
fill eclairs with the mixture. Sprinkle
with chopped parsley.

Steak and kidney pudding

Serves 4
8 oz   200 g   suet pastry
Filling
$1\frac{1}{2}$ lb   600 g   stewing steak
4 oz   100 g   pig's kidney
1 Tbs   1 Tbs   flour
1 tsp   1 tsp   salt
$\frac{1}{2}$ tsp $\frac{1}{2}$ tsp   black pepper
$\frac{1}{4}$ pint   125 ml stock or water

*$1\frac{1}{2}$ pint (750 ml) pudding basin
Preparation time about 25 min
excluding pastry making
Cooking time $3\frac{1}{2}$ hours*
Make the pastry (see method page 98).
Line the basin as shown on page 98.
Wipe the meat and cut into small
pieces ; wash the kidney and cut into
small pieces, removing the core and
membranes.
Mix the flour, salt and pepper
together, add the meat and toss well
so that it is completely coated. Pack
into the lined basin.
Add the stock or water and cover the
pudding as shown on page 98.
Lower into a steamer or pan half filled
with water, cover with a tight fitting
lid and cook for $3\frac{1}{2}$ hours.

Variation 1: Add 4 oz (100 g) small
whole mushrooms.
2: Add 4 oz (100 g) soaked and par-
boiled haricot beans.

Veal and ham pie

Serves 4-6

8 oz	200 g	hot water crust pastry

Filling

1 lb	400 g	pie veal
6 oz	150 g	bacon
2 tsp	2 tsp	chopped parsley
1 tsp	1 tsp	dried thyme
2	2	hard boiled eggs
1 Tbs	1 Tbs	milk
1 tsp	1 tsp	gelatine
¼ pint	125 ml	chicken stock or water

*Preparation time about 30 min
excluding pastry making
Cooking time 2 hours 400°F (220°C)
then 325°F (160°C)*

Make the pastry (see method page 99).
Line a 6 in cake tin with two-thirds of
it as shown on page 99.
Mince the veal, season well with salt
and black pepper.
Derind the bacon and mince finely,
mix with the veal, parsley and thyme.
Halve the eggs.
Pack half the mixture into the lined
tin, add the halved eggs and cover
with the remaining meat. Cover the
pie with the rest of the pastry (see
page 99), make a small hole in the
top and brush with the milk. Bake at
the higher temperature for 30 minutes.
Reduce to the lower temperature
and cook for a further 1½ hours.
Dissolve the gelatine in the stock, and
leave to cool.
Cool the pie and when the stock is
beginning to set pour into the pie.
Leave until firm before cutting.

Variation: Little pork pies. Mould the
paste in four small tins. Fill with minced
pork and sausagemeat layers. Bake at
the higher temperature for 30 minutes
and then for 1 hour at the lower
temperature.

Game pie

Serves 4-6

12 oz	300 g	hot water crust pastry

Filling

1	1	pheasant
2	2	pigeons
1 lb	400 g	veal
1 tsp	1 tsp	salt
½ tsp	½ tsp	black pepper
1 Tbs	1 Tbs	chopped chives
¼ pint	125 ml	stock (from bones)
1 tsp	1 tsp	gelatine
1	1	egg

*Preparation time about 35 min
excluding pastry making
Cooking time 2 hours 400°F (200°C)
then 325°F (170°C)*

Make the pastry (see method page 99).
Line a pie mould or 6 in (15 cm) cake
tin as shown on page 99.
Skin and bone the pheasant and
pigeons, cutting the flesh into small
pieces.
Boil up the bones in 2 pints (1 litre)
water to make stock for later use.
Mince the veal and put half in the base
of the lined tin, season well with salt
and pepper, place the game on top,
season well, and cover with the
remaining veal.
Cover the pie as shown on page 99,
make a hole in the top, and bake at the
higher temperature for 30 minutes.
Reduce to the lower temperature and
cook for a further 1½ hours.
Beat the egg and brush the top of the
pie 30 minutes before the end of the
cooking time.
Strain the stock and heat gently with
the gelatine, stirring until the gelatine
dissolves. Cool.
Remove the pie from the tin and, when
cold, pour in the stock.
Leave until set, preferably the next day,
before cutting.

Dundee cake

10 oz	250 g	currants and sultanas
2 oz	50 g	glacé cherries
2 oz	50 g	chopped mixed peel
1	1	orange
6 oz	150 g	butter
6 oz	150 g	castor sugar
4	4	eggs
4 oz	100 g	self raising flour
4 oz	100 g	plain flour
a pinch of		salt
2 oz	50 g	blanched almonds

7 in (18 cm) round cake tin
Preparation time about 20 min
Cooking time 2 hours 325°F (160°C)
Prepare the cake tin (see page 100).
Clean the currants and sultanas.
Grate the orange rind.
Chop the cherries and mix with the peel, orange rind, currants and sultanas.
Make a 'creamed' mixture (see method page 100) adding the mixed fruit and peel alternately with the flours.
Turn into the tin and smooth the top.
Split the almonds and arrange them evenly over the top of the cake.
Bake for 2 hours.
Leave in the tin to cool.

Victoria sandwich

6 oz	150 g	butter
6 oz	150 g	castor sugar
3	3	eggs
a pinch of		salt
6 oz	150 g	self raising flour
Filling		
2 Tbs	2 Tbs	seedless jam
1 oz	25 g	icing sugar

Two 7 in (18 cm) sandwich tins
Preparation time about 25 min
Cooking time 25 min 375°F (190°C)
Make a 'creamed' mixture (see method page 100).

Divide the mixture between the greased tins, spread evenly and bake for 25 minutes.
Reverse the tins after 15 minutes.
Cool on a wire rack.
Melt the jam and spread over one of the cakes. Sandwich them together. Sprinkle the top with sifted icing sugar.

Variation: Queen cakes. Add 2 oz (50 g) currants to the mixture and divide between 18 paper cases in bun tins. Bake for 20 minutes.

Christmas cake 1

1 lb	400 g	currants
1 lb	400 g	sultanas
1 lb	400 g	raisins
1	1	lemon
2 oz	50 g	blanched almonds
8 oz	100 g	chopped mixed peel
2 tsp	2 tsp	rosewater
4 Tbs	4 Tbs	brandy
1 lb	400 g	butter
1 lb	400 g	soft brown sugar
1 lb	400 g	plain flour
1 tsp	1 tsp	mixed spice
8	8	eggs

10 in (25 cm) square cake tin, or 11 in (28 cm) round tin
Preparation time about 25 min
Cooking time 4½ hours 300°F (150°C)

Clean the currants, sultanas and raisins.
Grate the lemon rind.
Chop the almonds finely and add to the fruit with the lemon rind and the mixed peel. Mix in the rosewater and brandy.
Make a 'creamed' mixture (see method page 100) sifting the spice with the flour and adding alternately with the fruit mixture.
Grease and line the tin (see page 103) for square tin or page 100 for round tin).
Turn the mixture into the prepared tin and smooth the top.

Bake for 4½ hours.
Cover the top of the cake with a layer of thick paper half way through cooking.
Leave the cake in the tin until cold.
Cover with almond paste, leave for 1 week before coating with icing.

Christmas cake 2

2 lb	1 Kg	mixed dried fruit
4 oz	100 g	glacé cherries
4 oz	100 g	mixed chopped peel
4 oz	100 g	ground almonds
4 Tbs	4 Tbs	sherry
1	1	lemon
8 oz	200 g	butter
8 oz	200 g	soft brown sugar
4	4	eggs
2 Tbs	2 Tbs	black treacle
6 oz	150 g	plain flour
6 oz	150 g	self raising flour
a pinch of		bicarbonate of soda
a pinch of		salt
1 tsp	1 tsp	mixed spice

9 in (22 cm) square cake tin
Preparation time about 30 min
Cooking time 3 hours 300°F (150°C)
Prepare the cake tin (see page 103).
Put the fruit into a large bowl.
Chop the cherries and grate the lemon rind. Add these to the fruit with the peel, almonds and sherry.
Make a 'creamed' mixture with the rest of the ingredients (see method page 100) beating in the treacle with the eggs, sifting the soda, salt and spice with the flour and adding alternately with the prepared fruit mixture.
Turn into the prepared tin and smooth the top.
Bake for 3 hours.
Leave in the tin until cold.
Cover with almond paste and leave for 1 week before icing.

Almond paste

1 lb	400 g	castor sugar
1 lb	400 g	icing sugar
2 lb	1 Kg	ground almonds
2	2	lemons
4	4	eggs
1 tsp	1 tsp	almond essence
1 tsp	1 tsp	orange flower water
1 tsp	1 tsp	vanilla essence

Preparation time about 30 min
including covering the cake
Sift the sugars together and mix with the almonds.
Squeeze the lemons.
Add the lemon juice, eggs and flavourings. Knead together until it forms a smooth paste.
Roll out ⅔ of the paste ½ in thick to fit the top of the cake.
Brush with apricot jam and place the cake upside down on top.
Roll out the remaining paste to a strip deep and long enough to cover the sides of the cake. Brush with apricot jam and press into position.
Turn the cake over, neaten the top edge and leave covered for 1 week to harden the paste before icing.

Royal icing

2 lb	1 Kg	icing sugar
3	3	egg whites
4 Tbs	4 Tbs	lemon juice
1 tsp	1 tsp	glycerine

Preparation time about 30 min
including covering the cake
Sift the sugar twice.
Beat the egg whites until smooth, add to the sugar with the lemon juice and glycerine.
Beat well until the icing is smooth and absolutely white.
Spread over the almond paste and peak with a fork or knife. Decorate.

above Sponge drops
opposite Coconut macaroons,
Small meringues,
Swiss roll, and Macaroons

Swiss roll

2	2	eggs
2 oz	50 g	castor sugar
2 oz	50 g	plain flour

Swiss roll tin approximately
11 in by 7 in (28 cm by 18 cm)
Preparation time about 15 min
Cooking time 10 min 400°F (200°C)
Line the tin with greaseproof paper
(see page 101).
Make a 'whisked' mixture (see method
page 101).
Pour into the prepared tin and
smooth the top.
Bake for 10 minutes.
Finish as shown on page 101.

Sponge cake

3	3	eggs
3 oz	75 g	castor sugar
3 oz	75 g	plain flour

6 in (15 cm) round cake tin
Preparation time about 20 min
Cooking time 40 min 350°F (180°C)
Grease the tin and dust liberally with
castor sugar.
Make a 'whisked' mixture (see method
page 101).
Pour into the prepared tin, and smooth
the top.
Bake for 40 minutes.
Cool in the tin slightly before turning on
to a wire rack.
Serve sliced with stewed fruit and cream.

Variation: Strawberry shortcake.
Add 1 oz (25 g) ground almonds and
1 Tbs water to the sponge mixture.
cook in three 6 in (15 cm) sandwich
tins. Sandwich together with 1 lb
(400 g) washed and sliced strawberries
and $\frac{1}{2}$ pint (250 ml) whipped cream.
Dust the top with icing sugar and
serve very cold.

Sponge drops

Makes 24

3	3	eggs
3 oz	75 g	castor sugar
3 oz	75 g	plain flour
Icing		
4 oz	100 g	icing sugar
1 tbs	1 tbs	cocoa

Preparation time about 15 min
Cooking time 7 min 375°F (190°C)
Make a 'whisked' mixture (see method page 101).
Drop spoonfuls well apart on the prepared baking tins.
Bake for 5 minutes.
Remove them immediately with a palette knife and cool on a wire rack.
Sift the icing sugar and cocoa together into a small bowl ; stir in enough water to make a soft icing ; beat well until smooth.
Stand the bowl over a pan of hot water and stir until the icing shines.
Dip the drops half into the icing and leave to harden on waxed paper.

Tip: A small knob of butter beaten into the icing speeds up the glossy appearance.

Macaroons

Makes 18

4 oz	100 g	ground almonds
8 oz	200 g	castor sugar
2	2	egg whites
2 tsp	2 tsp	ground rice
a few drops of		orange flower water
1 Tbs	1 Tbs	water
18	18	blanched almonds

Rice paper
Preparation time about 15 min
Cooking time 25 min 300°F (150°C)
Place the rice paper on baking tins.
Work all the ingredients, except the whole almonds, together until smooth.
Place spoonfuls of the mixture on the prepared tins, flatten each and place an almond in the centre.
Bake for 25 minutes.
Tear off excess paper, leaving a round underneath each macaroon.

Coconut macaroons

Makes 16

2	2	egg whites
4 oz	100 g	castor sugar
3½ oz	90 g	fine desiccated coconut
8	8	glacé cherries

Rice paper
Preparation time about 10 min
Cooking time 25 min 300°F (150°C)
Whisk the egg whites until stiff and standing in peaks.
Fold in the sugar and coconut ; mix well.
Spoon on to the prepared tins, and place ½ a cherry in the centre of each.
Bake for 25 minutes.
Remove excess paper and cool on a wire rack.

Small meringues

Makes 12

2	2	egg whites
2 oz	50 g	castor sugar
2 oz	50 g	granulated sugar
Filling		
½ pint	250 ml	double cream
a few drops		vanilla essence

Forcing bag and star nozzle
Preparation time about 20 min
Cooking time 6 hours 200°F (100°C)
Make a 'meringue' mixture (see method page 102).
Put the mixture into the forcing bag fitted with a star nozzle and pipe 24 small stars as shown on page 102.
Bake for 6 hours. Turn off the heat

and leave the meringues to cool in the oven.
Whip the cream and vanilla essence together until thick.
Sandwich the meringues together with cream and serve.

Tip: The meringues can be kept in an airtight tin for up to 3 months. Store the tin in a cool airy place.

Variation: Meringue glacé.
Pipe the mixture into large swirls and bake for up to 8 hours. Sandwich them together in pairs with ice cream. Decorate the top with whipped cream and a glacé cherry.

Gingerbread

4 oz	100 g	butter
2 oz	50 g	syrup
2 oz	50 g	treacle
4 oz	100 g	soft brown sugar
8 oz	200 g	plain flour
a pinch of		salt
1 tsp	1 tsp	ground ginger
1 tsp	1 tsp	cinnamon
½ tsp	½ tsp	bicarbonate of soda
2	2	eggs

8 in (20 cm) square cake tin
Preparation time about 15 min
Cooking time 1 hour 300°F (150°C)
Prepare the tin (see page 103).
Make a 'melted' mixture (see method page 103).
Pour into the tin.
Bake for 1 hour.
Leave in the tin for 10 minutes before turning on to a wire rack to cool.
Store for 1 week before cutting.

Tip: The gingerbread may be iced with a little glacé icing (see *Simnel cake* page 60) when cut into squares. Decorate with a small piece of stem ginger on each cake.

Scotch crispies

Makes 24

4 oz	100 g	butter
4 Tbs	4 Tbs	treacle
2 oz	50 g	castor sugar
2 oz	50 g	self raising flour
8 oz	200 g	rolled oats
a pinch of		salt
½ tsp	½ tsp	bicarbonate of soda

Shallow tin 9 in by 11 in (22 cm by 28 cm)
Preparation time about 10 min
Cooking time 40 min 350°F (180°C)
Make a 'melted' mixture (see method page 103) sifting the bicarbonate of soda with the dry ingredients.
Mix well and press into the prepared tin. Smooth the top.
Bake for 40 minutes.
Mark into 24 squares or fingers immediately and break when cold.

Gingernuts

Makes 20

2 oz	50 g	butter
2 Tbs	2 Tbs	syrup
4 oz	100 g	self raising flour
2 tsp	2 tsp	castor sugar
2 tsp	2 tsp	ground ginger
1 tsp	1 tsp	cinnamon
½ tsp	½ tsp	bicarbonate of soda

Preparation time about 10 min
Cooking time 15 min 350°F (180°C)
Make a 'melted' mixture (see method page 103) sifting the bicarbonate of soda with the dry ingredients. Cool, and knead the mixture until smooth.
Divide into 20 pieces and shape each into a ball.
Place well apart on greased baking tins; flatten slightly.
Bake for 20 minutes, reversing the trays after 15 minutes.
Cool on a wire rack.

Digestive biscuits

Makes 28

5 oz	125 g	self raising flour
½ tsp	½ tsp	salt
4 oz	100 g	butter
3 oz	75 g	medium oatmeal
1 oz	25 g	castor sugar
2 Tbs	2 Tbs	milk

Preparation time about 10 min
Cooking time 15 min 375°F (190°C)
Make a 'rubbed-in' mixture (see method page 104) adding the oatmeal with the sugar, and mixing to a stiff paste with the milk.
Roll out to ¼ in thick, prick the surface and cut out 28 rounds using a 2 in (5 cm) cutter, as shown on page 104.
Place on a baking tin and bake for 20 minutes. Reverse the trays after 15 minutes.
Cool on a wire rack.

Lunch loaf

12 oz	300 g	self raising flour
a pinch of		salt
6 oz	150 g	butter
3 oz	75 g	castor sugar
1	1	lemon
4 oz	100 g	sultanas
2 oz	50 g	glacé cherries
2	2	eggs
2 Tbs	2 Tbs	milk

2 lb (1 kg) loaf tin
Preparation time about 20 min
Cooking time 1 hour 375°F (190°C)
Chop the cherries. Grate the lemon rind.
Make a 'rubbed-in' mixture (see method page 104) adding the lemon rind, sultanas and cherries with the sugar.
Turn the mixture into a greased tin, smooth the top.
Bake for 1 hour.
Cool in the tin for 10 minutes before turning onto a wire rack.

opposite top Scones
opposite bottom Gingerbread,
Gingernuts, and Scotch crispies
below Lunch loaf, Raspberry buns,
Walnut cookies, and Digestive biscuits

Rock cakes

Makes 12

8 oz	200 g	self raising flour
a pinch of		salt
4 oz	100 g	butter
3 oz	75 g	castor sugar
3 oz	75 g	cleaned currants
1 oz	25 g	chopped mixed peel
1	1	egg
2 Tbs	2 Tbs	milk

Preparation time about 20 min
Cooking time 15 min 425°F (220°C)
Make a 'rubbed-in' mixture (see method page 104), adding the fruit and peel with the sugar.
Drop spoonfuls of the mixture on to greased baking tins.
Bake for 15 minutes.
Cool on a wire rack.

Variations 1: Hermits. Add ½ tsp each of cinnamon and nutmeg and an extra Tbs milk.
2: Raspberry buns. Spoon the mixture on to greased tins, make a small dent on the top of each, and place a small dab of raspberry jam in the centre of each.

Walnut cookies

Makes 20

4 oz	100 g	plain flour
a pinch of		salt
½ tsp	½ tsp	cinnamon
2 oz	50 g	butter
1 oz	25 g	soft brown sugar
2 oz	50 g	walnuts
1	1	egg
1 oz	25 g	glacé cherries

Preparation time about 15 min
Cooking time 10 min 400°F (200°C)
Chop the walnuts finely.
Make a 'rubbed-in' mixture (see method page 104) sifting the cinnamon

with the flour and salt and adding the walnuts with the sugar.
Divide the mixture into 20 and shape each into a ball.
Place on a greased baking tray, cut the cherries into small pieces and place a piece on each cookie.
Bake for 10 minutes.
Cool on a wire rack.

Scones

Makes 12

8 oz	200 g	self raising flour
½ tsp	½ tsp	salt
2 oz	50 g	butter
1 tsp	1 tsp	castor sugar
¼ pint	125 ml	milk

Preparation time about 10 min
Cooking time 10 min 450°F (230°C)
Make a 'rubbed-in' mixture (see method page 104), kneading to a smooth dough with the fingertips.
Roll out to ½ in thick and cut out 12 rounds using a 2 in (5 cm) plain cutter (see page 104).
Place them on a baking tin and bake for 10 minutes. Reverse trays, if making double quantity, after 6-7 minutes.
Cool on a wire rack. Serve with jam and cream.

Variations 1: Sultana. Add 1 oz (25 g) cleaned sultanas to the flour before mixing.
2: Cheese. Omit the sugar and use only 1 oz (25 g) butter. Add 2 oz (50 g) grated cheese and a pinch of cayenne pepper to the flour.
3: Brown treacle. Use wholemeal flour instead of plain white. Replace 2 Tbs of the milk with treacle.

Bread and Buns

The cooking times and temperatures given with these recipes are intended only as a guide. Experience will show whether your tastes require slight adjustments to the length of time or degree of heat required.

Points to remember
☐ The tepid temperature needed for the liquid in all yeast recipes can be achieved by mixing two parts of cold with one of boiling.
☐ The time required for the dough to double its bulk will vary a lot according to the warmth of the room. If in doubt the dough can be gently pressed with a forefinger — if it springs back immediately it is ready to be kneaded again and shaped as required by the recipe.
☐ To test if bread is cooked, turn out of the tin and knock the bottom. If it sounds hollow, it is done.
☐ Do not store bread until it has become quite cold.

White bread

3 lb	1½ Kg	plain flour
4 tsp	4 tsp	salt
2 oz	50 g	lard
1 oz	26 g	fresh yeast
1 tsp	1 tsp	castor sugar
1½ pint	750ml	water

Preparation time about 20 min plus proving time
Cooking time 50 min 425°F (220°C)
Make a dough mixture (see method page 105).
Divide the dough into six pieces, knead lightly and shape into oblongs to fit six 1 lb tins or three 2 lb tins.
Prove and bake for 50 minutes, reversing the tins after 35 minutes.
Cool on a wire rack.

Wholemeal bread

3 lb	1½ Kg	wholemeal flour
2 tsp	2 tsp	salt
4 oz	100 g	lard
1 oz	25 g	fresh yeast
1 tsp	1 tsp	castor sugar
1¾ pt	1 litre	water and milk mixed

Three 2 lb (1 kg) loaf tins
Preparation time about 20 min
plus proving time
Cooking time 55 min 425°F (220°C)
Make a dough mixture (see method
page 105).
Cover and leave until double its
original size.
Divide into three and knead each
piece lightly into an oblong.
Place in the greased tins and leave
covered until the dough reaches the
top of the tins.
Bake for 55 minutes reversing the tins
after 35 minutes.
Cool on a wire rack.

Tip: Wholemeal flour absorbs more
liquid than white flour; it may be
necessary to add 2-3 Tbs more when
mixing.

Variations: 1 Dinner rolls. Make up
1 lb dough using wholemeal flour
(see method page 105), and shape
each into a ball, or a plait as shown on
page 105. Place on greased baking tins,
and leave to prove. Brush with milk
and bake for 15 minutes at 425°F
(220°C), reversing the tins after
10 minutes. Cool on a wire rack.
2 Onion bread. Slice the cooked loaves
almost through to the base, and put
an onion ring between each slice.
Wrap each loaf in foil and bake for
about 10 minutes at 400°F (200°C).
Remove the foil and onion rings;
serve immediately.

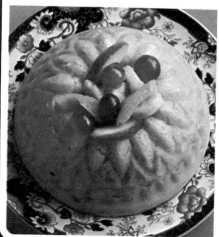

above Currant bread,
Chelsea buns, Hot cross buns,
and Cinnamon fruit ring
opposite top White bread,
Braided bread, and
Wholemeal bread
opposite bottom Savarin

9

Currant bread

1 lb	400 g	plain flour
1 tsp	1 tsp	salt
1 oz	25 g	butter
½ oz	12 g	fresh yeast
1 tsp	1 tsp	castor sugar
½ pt	250ml	milk
1	1	egg
4 oz	100 g	dried fruit
Glaze		
2 oz	50 g	castor sugar
4 Tbs	4 Tbs	water

Two 1 lb (400 g) loaf tins
Preparation time about 20 min plus proving time
Cooking time 40 min 375°F (190°C)
Make a dough mixture (see method page 105) adding the egg with the milk and the fruit after the butter has been rubbed in.
Cover and leave the dough to rise. Shape and prove in the tins.
Bake for 40 minutes.
Cool on a wire rack.
Dissolve the sugar in a pan with the water. Bring to the boil and cook for 2 minutes.
Brush the top of each loaf.

Braided bread

1 lb	400 g	plain flour
1 tsp	1 tsp	salt
2 oz	50 g	butter
½ oz	12 g	fresh yeast
1 tsp	1 tsp	castor sugar
½ pt	250ml	milk
Glaze		
1 Tbs	1 Tbs	milk
1 tsp	1 tsp	poppyseeds

Preparation time about 20 min plus proving time
Cooking time 45 min 425°F (220°C) then 375°F (190°C)
Make a dough mixture (see method page 105) adding the egg with the milk.
Cover and leave to double its bulk.
Knead lightly and divide into six pieces. Roll each into a sausage shape, making it thicker in the centre than at the ends.
Plait three strips together as shown on page 105, place on greased baking tins, cover and leave to prove.
Brush with the milk, and sprinkle with the poppyseeds.
Bake for 10 minutes at the higher temperature, reverse the trays and bake at the lower temperature for a further 35 minutes. Cool on a wire rack.

Chelsea buns

Makes 18

1 lb	400 g	plain flour
1 tsp	1 tsp	salt
3 oz	75 g	butter
3 oz	75 g	castor sugar
½ oz	12 g	fresh yeast
1 tsp	1 tsp	castor sugar
¼ pt	125ml	milk
2	2	eggs
Filling		
1 oz	25 g	melted lard
4 oz	100 g	currants
1 oz	25 g	castor sugar
Glaze		
1 Tbs	1 Tbs	syrup

Preparation time about 20 min plus proving time
Cooking time 25 min 425°F (220°C)
Make a dough mixture (see method page 105) adding the egg with the milk. Cover, and leave to double in bulk.
Roll into a rectangle 18 in by 12 in (45 cm by 30 cm).
Brush with lard and sprinkle with currants and sugar.
Roll up from the long side. Cut into 1½ in (4 cm) slices as shown on page 105.

Place in a shallow baking tin fairly close together. Leave to prove.
Bake for 25 minutes.
Heat the syrup and brush over the top of the buns. Remove them from the tin, break apart and cool on a wire rack.

Hot cross buns

Makes 12-14 buns

1 lb	400 g	plain flour
1 tsp	1 tsp	salt
1 tsp	1 tsp	mixed spice
6 oz	150 g	cleaned currants
2 oz	50 g	butter
½ oz	12 g	fresh yeast
1 tsp	1 tsp	castor sugar
½ pt	250ml	milk
1	1	egg
4 oz	100 g	shortcrust pastry

Glaze

2 oz	50 g	castor sugar
4 Tbs	4 Tbs	water

Preparation time about 20 min plus proving time
Cooking time 20 min 400°F (200°C)
Make a dough mixture (see method page 105) sifting the spice with the flour and salt, and adding the egg with the milk.
Cover and leave to double its bulk.
Divide into 12 pieces and shape each into a ball ; place on a baking tin, cover and leave to prove.
Roll out the pastry and cut into very thin strips.
Brush the top of the buns with milk and place two strips of pastry across the top to represent a cross as shown on page 105.
Bake for 20 minutes.
Cool on a wire rack.
Make up the glaze as for *Currant bread* (page 76) and brush the buns, but leave the pastry clear.
Serve hot with butter.

Cinnamon fruit ring

1 lb	400 g	plain flour
½ tsp	½ tsp	salt
2 oz	50 g	butter
½ oz	12 g	fresh yeast
½ pt	250ml	milk
1	1	egg

Filling

1 Tbs	1 Tbs	melted butter
2 oz	50 g	soft brown sugar
4 oz	100 g	mixed dried fruit
1 tsp	1 tsp	cinnamon

Glaze

2 oz	50 g	castor sugar
4 Tbs	4 Tbs	water

Preparation time about 20 min plus proving time
Cooking time 20 min 425°F (220°C)
Make a dough mixture (see method page 105) adding the egg with the milk.
Cover and leave to double its bulk.
Knead lightly and roll out to an oblong about 18 in by 8 in (45 cm by 20 cm).
Brush with melted butter and sprinkle with sugar, fruit and cinnamon.
Roll up from the long side, dampen the ends and press together to form a circle.
Place the circle on a greased baking tin.
Using a sharp knife, cut almost through the roll from the outer edge to the centre, at 1½ in (4 cm) intervals. Twist the slices so that they lie flat.
Bake for 20 minutes.
Cool on a wire rack.
Make the glaze as for *Currant bread* (page 76) brush over the ring and leave to cool.

Savarin

½ oz	12 g	fresh yeast
1 tsp	1 tsp	castor sugar
¼ pt	125ml	warm milk
8 oz	200 g	plain flour
a pinch of		salt
2	2	eggs
3 oz	75 g	softened butter
3 oz	75 g	blanched almonds
Glaze		
2 oz	50 g	castor sugar
2 Tbs	2 Tbs	water
1 Tbs	1 Tbs	rum

1½ pint (1 litre) ring mould
Preparation time about 20 min
plus proving time
Cooking time 20 min 425°F (220°C)
Cream the yeast and sugar together in a large bowl. Add the milk, mix well and stir in the flour and salt. Leave until the mixture begins to froth.
Beat the eggs and butter together until smooth, add to the yeast mixture and beat together until smooth.
Shred the almonds and sprinkle over the base and sides of the greased mould.
Pour in the batter and leave in a warm place until it reaches the top of the tin.
Bake for 20 minutes.
Dissolve the sugar in a small pan with the water, bring to the boil and boil for 1 minute. Add the rum and pour over the savarin immediately.
Serve with glacé fruits or fresh fruit salad.

Variation: Rum babas. Make up mixture as above, omitting the almonds, and adding 1 oz (25 g) each of raisins, currants, and mixed chopped peel with the egg and butter mixture. Half fill 16 dariole moulds, leave to rise to the tops, and bake for 12 minutes at 400°F (200°C). Make the syrup as for savarin, turn the babas on to a hot plate and pour the syrup over immediately. Serve with whipped cream.

Doughnuts

Makes 12		
1 lb	400 g	plain flour
a pinch of		salt
2 oz	50 g	butter
½ oz	12 g	fresh yeast
1 tsp	1 tsp	castor sugar
½ pt	250ml	milk
1	1	egg
Filling		
4 oz	100 g	jam
Coating		
4 oz	100 g	castor sugar
1 tsp	1 tsp	cinnamon

Deep fat frying pan, basket and oil
Preparation time about 30 min
plus proving time
Cooking time 10 min
Make a dough mixture (see method page 105) adding the egg with the milk.
Cover and leave to double its bulk.
Divide the dough into 12 portions. Shape each into a ball, make a hole in the centre of each and fill with jam. Pinch the edges together to seal.
Place on a greased tray and leave to prove.
Heat the oil to 375°F (190°C) and fry the doughnuts three or four at a time for 10 minutes, turning them constantly in the fat to brown evenly.
Mix the sugar and cinnamon together on a sheet of foil or greaseproof paper and toss the doughnuts in it whilst they are still hot.
Cool and serve.

10

Puddings

The cooking times and temperatures given with these recipes are intended only as a guide. Experience will show whether your tastes require slight adjustments to the length of time or degree of heat required.

Fruit tart

Serves 4

12 oz	300 g	shortcrust pastry
1½ lb	600 g	apples
2 oz	50 g	castor sugar

Glaze

2 Tbs	2 Tbs	milk
1 Tbs	1 Tbs	granulated sugar

8 in (20 cm) pie plate
Preparation time about 25 min
Cooking time 40 min 425°F (220°C)
then 350°F (180°C)

Make the pastry (see method page 92). **Roll** it out to an oblong 16 in by 8 in (40 cm by 20 cm). Cut in half to make two 8 in (20 cm) squares and line the plate with one of them.
Peel and core the apples, slice into the lined plate, and sprinkle with sugar.
Moisten the edges of the pastry and place the other square on top. Press the edges together to seal.
Trim the edges, flake and flute them (see page 92).
Make a small hole in the top. Brush the top with milk and sprinkle with granulated sugar.
Bake for 20 minutes at the higher temperature. Reduce temperature and cook for a further 20 minutes.
Serve warm with cream or custard.

Variation: Apple amber. Line the sides of a 1½ pint (750 ml) pie dish with shortcrust pastry. Fill the dish with pre-cooked apples, beaten to a pulp with the yolks of 2 eggs and 2 oz (50 g) soft brown sugar. Bake for 30 minutes as for fruit tart. Cover with meringue made with two egg whites and 2 oz (50 g) castor sugar (see method page 102) and bake for a further 5 minutes to brown the meringue.

Baked custard

Serves 4

1 pint	500 ml	milk
2 oz	50 g	castor sugar
4	4	eggs

1½ pint (750 ml) pie dish or cake tin
Preparation time about 15 minutes
Cooking time 1½ hours 275°F (140°C)
Heat the milk gently until almost boiling.
Beat the sugar and eggs together until smooth and creamy. Beat in the milk.
Strain into the greased dish or cake tin.
Stand the dish or tin in a roasting tin half filled with hot water.
Bake in the centre of the oven for 1½ hours.
Serve warm with fruit.

Variation: Caramel custard.
Dissolve 3 oz (75g) castor sugar in 1 Tbs water in a small pan. Bring to the boil and boil until the syrup begins to turn golden brown. Pour into the tin and coat the base and sides.
Pour the custard into the mould over the back of a spoon to prevent it from breaking the caramel.
Bake as for baked custard.

Treacle layer

Serves 4

8 oz	200 g	suet pastry
1 tsp	1 tsp	cinnamon
4 Tbs	4 Tbs	syrup

1¼ pint (625 ml.) pudding basin
Preparation time about 15 min
excluding pastry making
Cooking time 2 hours
Make the pastry (see method page 98) adding the cinnamon with the flour.
Divide into three, and shape into rounds to fit the basin.
Place ⅓ of the treacle in the bottom of the greased basin, and cover with a layer of pastry. Continue to fill the dish with alternate layers of syrup and dough, finishing with a layer of pastry.
Cover the basin with greased foil or greaseproof paper (see page 98).
Steam for 2 hours, topping up the pan with boiling water if necessary.
Serve hot with custard or cream.

Fairy pudding

Serves 4

½ pint	250 ml	water
1	1	lemon
4 oz	100 g	castor sugar
1½ Tbs	1½ Tbs	cornflour
2	2	egg whites

1 pint (500 ml) mould
Preparation time about 15 min
Cooking time 5 min
Grate the lemon rind and squeeze the juice.
Heat the water, lemon rind, juice and sugar gently until the sugar has dissolved.
Bring to the boil and boil for 2-3 minutes.
Mix the cornflour to a smooth paste with a little water and add to the syrup, stirring all the time to prevent lumps. Cook for 2-3 minutes.
Whisk the egg whites until stiff and standing in peaks.
Pour the cornflour mixture on to the egg whites, whisking all the time.
Pour the mixture immediately into the wetted mould and leave in a cool place until set.
Turn out and serve with cream.

Tip: A few drops of green colouring can be added.

Eve's pudding

Serves 4

3	3	cooking apples
2 oz	50 g	castor sugar
2 oz	50 g	butter
1	1	egg
2 oz	50 g	self raising flour

1½ pint (750 ml) pie dish
Preparation time about 20 min
Cooking time 30 min 400°F (200°C)
Peel and core the apples, slice and place in a heavy based pan with 1 Tbs water. Cover and stew gently for 5 minutes.
Turn them into the greased pie dish.
Make a 'creamed' mixture (see method page 100) with the remaining ingredients.
Spread the mixture on top of the apples.
Bake for 30 minutes.
Serve warm with cream or custard.

Variation: Stir 2 oz (50 g) chopped glacé cherries into the cake mixture with the flour.

Boiled fruit pudding

Serves 4

8 oz	200 g	suet pastry
2 lb	1 kg	cooking apples
2 oz	50 g	castor sugar
4	4	cloves

1½ pint (750 ml) pudding basin
Preparation time about 20 min
excluding pastry making
Cooking time 1½ hours
Make the pastry (see method page 98) Roll it out and line the greased pudding basin (see page 98).
Peel, core and slice the apples, and pack the slices into the lined basin.
Sprinkle with the sugar and cloves.
Cover the pie with the remaining pastry, and then with greased foil (see page 98). Boil or steam for 1½ hours, topping up with boiling water throughout if necessary. Serve with cornflour sauce (See *Sponge pudding with cornflour sauce* page 86).

Queen of puddings

Serves 4

1	1	lemon
1 pint	500 ml	milk
1 oz	25 g	castor sugar
6 oz	150 g	fresh white breadcrumbs
2 oz	50 g	butter
2	2	egg yolks
Topping		
3 Tbs	3 Tbs	raspberry jam
2 oz	50 g	castor sugar
2	2	egg whites

1½ pint (750 ml) pie dish
Preparation time about 25 min
Cooking time 45 min 350°F (180°C)
Thinly pare the rind of the lemon, and put into a pan with the milk. Heat gradually until almost boiling.
Put the sugar, breadcrumbs and butter into a bowl, strain over the milk and beat until smooth.
Add the yolks to the bread mixture and beat well.
Pour into the prepared dish and bake in the centre of the oven for 30 minutes.
Spread the jam over the top of the pudding.
Make a meringue mixture (see method page 102) with the egg whites and sugar.
Pile or pipe the meringue on top of the jam (see page 102) and continue baking for a further 15 minutes.

Rice pudding

Serves 4

2 oz	50 g	pudding rice
1 oz	25 g	castor sugar
a pinch of		salt
1 pint	500 ml	milk
½ oz	12 g	butter
a pinch of		grated nutmeg

$1\frac{1}{4}$ *pint (625 ml) pie dish*
Preparation time about 5 min
Cooking time $2\frac{1}{2}$ *hours 300°F (150°C)*
Grease the dish and put the rice,
sugar and salt in.
Add the milk. Dot with small pieces of
the butter and sprinkle with nutmeg.
Bake in the centre of the oven for
$2\frac{1}{2}$ hours.

Tips: Stirring the skin into the pudding
during cooking will give a thicker,
creamier result.
2. Replace half the milk with
evaporated milk for a creamier pudding.

Baked apple dumplings

Serves 4

12 oz	300 g	shortcrust pastry
4	· 4	cooking apples
2 Tbs	2 Tbs	soft brown sugar
4	4	cloves

Preparation time about 15 min
Cooking time 40 min 425°F (220°C)
Make the pastry (see method page 92).
Roll it out to a 12 in square, and cut
out four 6 in squares.
Peel and core the apples. Place one in
the centre of each square and fill with
the brown sugar and cloves.
Dampen the edges of the pastry and
bring the points together, pressing to
seal.
Bake for 40 minutes.
Serve warm with cream.

above Profiteroles
opposite top Christmas pudding,
Baked apple dumplings, and
Lemon meringue pie
opposite bottom Fruit tart

Christmas pudding

Makes 4 puddings
12 oz	300 g	plain flour
a pinch of		salt
1 tsp	1 tsp	ground ginger
1 tsp	1 tsp	cinnamon
1 tsp	1 tsp	ground nutmeg
1 lb	400 g	shredded suet
12 oz	300 g	fresh white breadcrumbs
1 lb	400 g	currants
1 lb	400 g	raisins
12 oz	300 g	soft brown sugar
12 oz	300 g	cooking apples
1	1	lemon
4	4	eggs
2 Tbs	2 Tbs	brandy

4 x 1¼ pint (625 ml) pudding basins
Preparation time about 30 min
Cooking time 8 hours
Sift the flour and salt and spices into a large bowl. Add the remaining dry ingredients and mix well.
Peel and grate the apples ; grate the lemon rind, and squeeze the juice. Add these to the mixture with the eggs and brandy. Beat well until evenly blended.
Put into the greased basins, cover with greased foil or greaseproof paper (see page 98) and steam for 8 hours, topping up the pan with boiling water as required.
Remove the foil or paper and recover with fresh foil.
Reboil for 3 hours when needed.
Serve with rum butter or hard sauce, dust the top with icing sugar.

Cumberland rum butter

4 oz	100 g	butter, unsalted
8 oz	200 g	pale brown soft sugar
2 Tbs	2 Tbs	brandy
a pinch of		cinnamon
a pinch of		grated nutmeg

Preparation time about 10 min

Cream the butter and sugar until light and fluffy.
Gradually beat in the brandy and spices. Beat until smooth.
Chill for 1 hour before serving with Christmas pudding.

Hard sauce

Makes ½ pint (250 ml)
1 Tbs	1 Tbs	cornflour
2 Tbs	2 Tbs	soft brown sugar
2 Tbs	2 Tbs	brandy or rum
½ pint	250 ml	milk
2 Tbs	2 Tbs	cream

Preparation time about 5 min
Cooking time 5 min
Mix the cornflour and sugar to a smooth paste with the brandy.
Heat the milk until boiling. Pour onto the cornflour paste, stirring to prevent lumps.
Bring back to the boil, stirring until thickened.
Serve hot with Christmas pudding.

Profiteroles

Serves 4-6
2½ oz	65 g	choux paste
Filling		
½ pint	250 ml	double cream
1 oz	25 g	castor sugar
Sauce		
2 oz	50 g	butter
1 Tbs	1 Tbs	syrup
2 Tbs	2 Tbs	cocoa powder
¼ pint	125 ml	water

Preparation time about 25 min
Cooking time 35 min 425°F (220°C)
then 350°F (180°C)
Make the pastry (see method page 97).
Spoon the choux paste on to greased and floured tins (see page 97).
Bake at the higher temperature for

20 minutes, reduce the heat and cook for a further 15 minutes.
Cool on a wire rack.
Whip the cream until thick, beat in the sugar.
When the choux buns are completely cold, slit along the side (see page 97) and fill with the cream mixture.
Melt the butter and syrup together, stir in the cocoa and cook for 2-3 minutes, stirring to prevent it sticking.
Add the water and bring to the boil, stirring until smooth. Cook gently for 5 minutes.
Pile the buns in a heatproof dish and pour the sauce over.
Serve immediately.

Variation: Cream buns. Use a dessert-spoon to spoon the mixture on to the baking tins. Bake for 45 minutes.
Fill with whipped cream sweetened with castor sugar and dust the tops of the buns with icing sugar.

Lemon meringue pie

Serves 4-6

8 oz	200 g	shortcrust or flan pastry

Filling

9 oz	225 g	castor sugar
3 oz	75 g	cornflour
¾ pint	375 ml	water
2	2	lemons
a pinch of		salt
3	3	egg yolks

Topping

3	3	egg whites
3 oz	75 g	castor sugar

8 in (20 cm) flan ring on a baking tin
Preparation time 30 min
Cooking time 45 min 425°F (220°C)
then 350°F (180°C)
Make the pastry (see method page 92 or 93).
Roll it out and line the flan ring (see page 93). Bake blind for 20 minutes.

To make the filling, mix the castor sugar and cornflour together with a little of the water to make a smooth paste. Grate the lemon rind, squeeze the juice, and add to the paste with the rest of the water and the salt.
Bring slowly to the boil, stirring until thickened.
Cool slightly, then beat in the egg yolks.
Put the mixture into the pastry case.
For the topping, make a meringue mixture (see method page 102).
Pipe or fork the meringue on top of the lemon filling (see page 102) and bake at the lower temperature for 20 minutes.

Variation: Orange meringue pie. Use grated rind and juice of 2 oranges instead of lemons.

Summer pudding

Serves 4-6

8	8	thick slices of fresh white bread
2 lb	1 Kg	fresh soft fruit
2 oz	50 g	castor sugar

1½ pint (750 ml) pudding basin
Preparation time about 30 min
Cooking time 5 min
Remove the crusts from the bread and cut into fingers.
Grease the basin and line with the bread.
Wash the fruit, put into a pan with the sugar and stew gently for 5 minutes or until the juice runs.
Pour into the lined basin, cover with the remaining bread and leave until cold.
Turn out on to a large serving dish and serve very cold with whipped cream.

Sponge pudding with cornflour sauce

Serves 4

4 oz	100 g	butter
4 oz	100 g	castor sugar
2	2	eggs
4 oz	100 g	self raising flour
a pinch of		salt

Sauce

1 Tbs	1 Tbs	cornflour
1 Tbs	1 Tbs	cocoa powder
2 Tbs	2 Tbs	castor sugar
1 pint	500 ml	milk

$1\frac{1}{4}$ pint (625 ml) pudding basin
Preparation time about 25 min
Cooking time $1\frac{1}{2}$ hours

Make a 'creamed' mixture (see method page 100).

Turn into the greased basin, cover with greased foil (see page 98), and steam for $1\frac{1}{2}$ hours, topping up the pan with boiling water if necessary.

Mix the cornflour, cocoa and castor sugar together with a little of the milk to make a smooth paste.

Heat the rest of the milk, pour on to the cornflour paste, stirring well to prevent lumps.

Return the mixture to the pan and bring to the boil, stirring until thickened.

Turn the pudding on to a hot plate, pour a little of the sauce over and hand the rest separately.

Variation 1: Castle puddings. Divide the mixture between $\frac{1}{4}$ pt (125 ml) basins. Steam for 25 minutes. Turn out and serve with jam sauce.
2: Raspberry pudding. Stir 2 oz (50 g) raspberry jam into the creamed mixture before adding the flour. Cook as for sponge pudding. Turn out and serve with plain cornflour sauce.
3: Black top pudding. Line the base of the basin with half a 10 oz (283.5 g) can blackcurrant pie filling. Heat the rest with 3 Tbs water and serve separately as a sauce.

Spotted dick with syrup sauce

Serves 4

8 oz	200 g	self raising flour
a pinch of		salt
4 oz	100 g	shredded suet
2 oz	50 g	currants
2 oz	50 g	raisins
2 oz	50 g	castor sugar
$\frac{1}{4}$ pt	125 ml	water

Sauce

2 Tbs	2 Tbs	syrup
$\frac{1}{2}$	$\frac{1}{2}$	lemon

Preparation time about 15 min
Cooking time $1\frac{1}{2}$ hours

Make a suet pastry mixture (see method page 98) adding the fruit and sugar with the suet.

Shape the dough into a sausage, and wrap it loosely in a floured cloth.
Cover with boiling water in a saucepan and boil for $1\frac{1}{2}$ hours, topping up with boiling water throughout, if necessary, to keep it covered.

Heat the syrup with the juice from the $\frac{1}{2}$ lemon.

Pour over the pudding, and serve.

NB The pudding can be cooked in a $1\frac{1}{2}$ pint (750 ml) basin instead of a cloth. To cover the basin, see page 98.

Variations 1: Date or fig. Use chopped dates or crystallised figs instead of currants and sultanas.
2: Cherry. Use glacé cherries instead of dried fruits, and add 1 tsp cinnamon to the flour before adding the water.
3: Lemon or orange. Add the grated rind and juice of 1 lemon or orange instead of the dried fruits.
4: Jam. Add 2 Tbs jam to the dough with the water, and omit the dried fruit.

Treacle tart

Serves 4

6 oz	150 g	flan pastry
5 Tbs	5 Tbs	syrup
4 Tbs	4 Tbs	breadcrumbs
a pinch of		ground ginger
½	½	lemon

8 in (20 cm) pie plate
Preparation time about 25 min
Cooking time 20 min 425°F (220°C)
Make the pastry (see method page 93).
Roll it out and line the pie plate. Trim
the edges, roll out the trimmings and
cut out thin strips. Keep them to one
side.
Mix the remaining ingredients
together with the juice from the lemon,
and pour into the lined plate.
Make a lattice pattern over the filling
with the strips of pastry.
Bake in the centre of the oven for
20 minutes. Serve with cream.

Baked Alaska

Serves 4-6

3	3	eggs
3 oz	75 g	castor sugar
3 oz	75 g	plain flour
Filling		
1 lb	400 g	block ice cream
Topping		
2	2	egg whites
4 oz	100 g	castor sugar

7 in (18 cm) sponge flan tin
Preparation time about 25 min
Cooking time 17 min 400°F (200°C)
Make a 'whisked' mixture (see method
page 101) with the first three ingredients.
Pour into the greased flan tin, and
smooth the top.
Bake for 15 minutes.
Cool on a wire rack.
Make a 'meringue' mixture with the
topping ingredients (see method page

102), and keep to one side.
Place the cool flan on a heatproof
dish, and put the block of ice cream in
the centre. Cut the ice cream to spread
it as evenly as possible over the whole
of the flan surface, but work quickly
so that the ice cream does not melt.
Spread the meringue over the ice
cream, making sure that it is completely
covered. Fork into peaks (see page
102). Bake for 2 minutes, or until the
meringue is tipped brown. Serve at
once.

Upside down pudding

Serves 4
Topping

15 oz	425.25 g	can pineapple slices
2 oz	50 g	butter
2 oz	50 g	soft brown sugar
Pudding		
3 oz	75 g	butter
3 oz	75 g	castor sugar
2	2	eggs
4 oz	100 g	self raising flour
a pinch of		salt
2 tsp	2 tsp	warm water
a few drops of		vanilla essence

7 in (18 cm) round cake tin
Preparation time about 20 min
Cooking time 40 min 375°F (190°C)
Drain and dry the pineapple. Cream
the butter and brown sugar until light
and fluffy.
Grease the tin and spread the butter
mixture over the base. Arrange the
pineapple on top.
Make a 'creamed' mixture (see
method page 100) with the remaining
ingredients, adding the vanilla essence
and water after the flour.
Spread the mixture evenly on top of
the pineapple and smooth the top.
Bake for 40 minutes. Invert on to a
warm serving plate and serve with
cream.

Autotimer Cookery

Automatic oven controls can be a great boon to the busy housewife, for they enable her to prepare meals in advance, and then to leave the control of the cooking to the automatic timer set to the necessary time and temperature. Many individual dishes as well as complete menus can be treated in this way, leaving the housewife free for other activities. Care must, of course, be taken in the selection of dishes to be cooked in this manner, because some mixtures are just not suitable to be left for long periods uncooked—dishes which include a wet mixture standing on uncooked shortcrust pastry, such as Fruit tart, come into this category. If you want to use these in automatic cookery, do so when the cooking is to be done a comparatively short time ahead.

Make sure that the dishes you select have the following characteristics – they cover the important differences between normal cookery and autotimer cookery.

1 The dishes must be suitable for starting off cold.

2 They must not be affected by being left uncooked at room temperature for some hours.

3 They must require no attention during cooking.

4 The dishes which are cooked together must require approximately the same oven temperature, and the same cooking times.

Within those limits, meals can be planned around the recipes used everyday in your home, and around many of the recipes in this book. The menus which follow are based on a selection of these recipes – use the index to find the pages on which individual recipes appear.

	Coq au vin	Baked onions	Baked custard
Time	2 hours	2 hours	2 hours
Position	Top	Centre	Low
Temperature	300 °F (150 °C)	300 °F (150 °C)	300 °F (150 °C)
Special Instructions		Cover with foil	Cover with foil
Serving Ideas	Plain boiled rice		Fresh canned fruit

	Baked ham slice	Jacket potatoes	Queen of puddings
Time	1½ hours	1½ hours	1½ hours
Position	Centre	Centre	Low/Floor
Temperature	350 °F (180 °C)	350 °F (180 °C)	350 °F (180 °C)
Special Instructions	Cover dish with lid or foil	Place around ham dish	Beat jam into mixture, pile meringue on top
Serving Ideas	green salad		

	Hot pot	Braised celery	Rice pudding
Time	2½ hours	2½ hours	2½ hours
Position	Top/Centre	Floor	Centre/Low
Temperature	350°F (180 °C)	350°F (180 °C)	350 °F (180 °C)
Special Instructions	Cover top layer of potatoes with melted fat		
Serving Ideas			Stewed fruit

	Soused herrings	Pineapple upside down pudding	
Time	1 hour	1 hour	
Position	Lower/Centre	Top/Centre	
Temperature	375°F (190°C)	375°F (190°C)	
Special Instructions	Cover fish with foil.		
Serving Ideas	Tomato salad and crisps.	Custard or cream	

	Stuffed fish	Duchesse potatoes	Treacle tart
Time	½ hour	½ hour	½ hour
Position	Low	Centre	Top
Temperature	400 °F (200 °C)	400 °F (200 °C)	400 °F (200 °C)
Special Instructions	Brush fish with melted butter.		
Serving Ideas	Broccoli		Cream or custard

	Shepherds' pie	Baked tomatoes	Chocolate souffles
Time	30 min	30 min	30 min
Position	Centre	Centre	Top
Temperature	375 °F (190 °C)	375 °F (190 °C)	375 °F (190 °C)
Special Instructions	Place on same shelf as tomatoes.	Put whole, washed tomatoes in shallow dish with little cold water. Cover with foil.	Divide mixture into 4 dishes.
Serving Ideas			White sauce flavoured with brandy.

	Roast shoulder of lamb	Roast potatoes	Carrots
Time	1½ hours	1½ hours	1½ hours
Position	Bottom/Floor	Bottom/Floor	Centre
Temperature	375 °F (190 °C)	375 °F (190 °C)	375 °F (190 °C)
Special Instructions		Coat potatoes with melted fat and cook with meat.	Dice carrots, cover with cold salted water. Cover dish.
Serving Ideas	Make gravy from juices (see page 17).		

	Fruit tart
Time	1½ hours
Position	Top
Temperature	375 °F (190 °C)

	Pork with apples and red cabbage	Steamed potatoes	Black top pudding
Time	2 hours	2 hours	2 hours
Position	Centre/Low	Low/Centre	Low/Centre
Temperature	350 °F (180 °C)	350 °F (180 °C)	350 °F (180 °C)
Special Instructions		Cut potatoes small and put in cold water. Cover dish with foil and cook on same shelf as pudding.	Stand dish in bain marie and cover top with foil.
Serving Ideas			Cream or custard

	Coq au vin	Baked onions	Baked custard
Time	2 hours	2 hours	2 hours
Position	Top	Centre	Low
Temperature	300 °F (150 °C)	300 °F (150 °C)	300 °F (150 °C)
Special Instructions		Cover with foil	Cover with foil
Serving Ideas	Plain boiled rice		Fresh canned fruit

	Baked ham slice	Jacket potatoes	Queen of puddings
Time	1½ hours	1½ hours	1½ hours
Position	Centre	Centre	Low/Floor
Temperature	350 °F (180 °C)	350 °F (180 °C)	350 °F (180 °C)
Special Instructions	Cover dish with lid or foil	Place around ham dish	Beat jam into mixture, pile meringue on top
Serving Ideas	green salad		

	Hot pot	Braised celery	Rice pudding
Time	2½ hours	2½ hours	2½ hours
Position	Top/Centre	Floor	Centre/Low
Temperature	350°F (180 °C)	350°F (180 °C)	350 °F (180 °C)
Special Instructions	Cover top layer of potatoes with melted fat		
Serving Ideas			Stewed fruit

	Soused herrings	Pineapple upside down pudding
Time	1 hour	1 hour
Position	Lower/Centre	Top/Centre
Temperature	375°F (190°C)	375°F (190°C)
Special Instructions	Cover fish with foil.	
Serving Ideas	Tomato salad and crisps.	Custard or cream

	Stuffed fish	Duchesse potatoes	Treacle tart
Time	½ hour	½ hour	½ hour
Position	Low	Centre	Top
Temperature	400 °F (200 °C)	400 °F (200 °C)	400 °F (200 °C)
Special Instructions	Brush fish with melted butter.		
Serving Ideas	Broccoli		Cream or custard

	Shepherds' pie	Baked tomatoes	Chocolate souffles
Time	30 min	30 min	30 min
Position	Centre	Centre	Top
Temperature	375 °F (190 °C)	375 °F (190 °C)	375 °F (190 °C)
Special Instructions	Place on same shelf as tomatoes.	Put whole, washed tomatoes in shallow dish with little cold water. Cover with foil.	Divide mixture into 4 dishes.
Serving Ideas			White sauce flavoured with brandy.

	Roast shoulder of lamb	Roast potatoes	Carrots
Time	1½ hours	1½ hours	1½ hours
Position	Bottom/Floor	Bottom/Floor	Centre
Temperature	375 °F (190 °C)	375 °F (190 °C)	375 °F (190 °C)
Special Instructions		Coat potatoes with melted fat and cook with meat.	Dice carrots, cover with cold salted water. Cover dish.
Serving Ideas	Make gravy from juices (see page 17).		

	Fruit tart
Time	1½ hours
Position	Top
Temperature	375°F (190°C)

	Pork with apples and red cabbage	Steamed potatoes	Black top pudding
Time	2 hours	2 hours	2 hours
Position	Centre/Low	Low/Centre	Low/Centre
Temperature	350 °F (180 °C)	350 °F (180 °C)	350 °F (180 °C)
Special Instructions		Cut potatoes small and put in cold water. Cover dish with foil and cook on same shelf as pudding.	Stand dish in bain marie and cover top with foil.
Serving Ideas			Cream or custard

Methods

The following 14 pages set out the steps which go to make up the basic mixtures used in cookery. All the recipes which use a basic method are referred to one or more of these pages, where we are able to illustrate each stage.

Many cooks, however experienced, find difficulty with one sort of recipe or another, and so tend to avoid some dishes. Others are quite simply 'put off' trying to make say bread, or choux pastry, because they feel there is some mystery attached to the processes involved. And of course for the learner cook there are hazards attached to the simplest recipes, because she just does not know how to start!

All these problems are solved on the following pages. There are step-by-step photographs to show you just how the mixtures should look; there are simple instructions to follow – and there are also pictures to illustrate other processes – lining cake tins, finishing a Swiss roll, piping eclairs . . . We are sure that you will find cooking a lot less involved with guesswork and costly time-consuming mistakes if you use these pages with care. Good luck, and happy cookery.

Shortcrust pastry

	8 oz pastry		4 oz pastry	
plain flour	8 oz	200 g	4 oz	100 g
lard/cooking fat	2 oz	50 g	1 oz	25 g
butter	2 oz	50 g	1 oz	25 g
salt	a pinch of		a pinch of	
water to mix	1½ Tbs	1½ Tbs	1 Tbs	1 Tbs

Preparation time about 10 min

Sift the flour and salt into a large bowl.
Add the fats cut into small pieces.
Rub in the fats with the fingertips until the mixture resembles fine breadcrumbs (**1**).
Add sufficient water to make a stiff paste (**2**).
Knead lightly until smooth (**3**).
Use as required.

What went wrong and why

Hard	Too much water
	Over handling
	Oven too cool
	Cooked too long
Soft	Too much fat
	Insufficient water
	Overcooked
Soggy	Oven too cool
	Undercooked
	Filling too wet (for pies)
Shrunken	Too much rolling has stretched the pastry
Blistered	Fat insufficiently rubbed in

Covering a pie dish
Roll the pastry out about 2 in. larger than the dish, and cut off three strips about 1 in. wide.

Brush the rim of the dish with water and fit the pastry strips round it, cutting to size. Brush again with water.

Lift the remaining pastry on the rolling pin and put it over the pie dish (**1**). Press the edges together, and cut away any surplus pastry with a knife (**2**). Flake the edge with the knife, held horizontally.

Flute the edge with the back of

the knife and tip of your thumb (**3**). Cut a hole in the centre of the pie and brush with beaten egg or water.

Flan pastry

	8 oz pastry		6 oz pastry	
plain flour	8 oz	200 g	6 oz	150 g
salt	a pinch of		a pinch of	
butter	4 oz	100 g	3 oz	75 g
castor sugar	1 oz	50 g	1 oz	25 g
egg	1	1		
egg yolk			1	1
water			2 tsp	2 tsp

Preparation time about 10 min
Sift the flour and salt into a large bowl.
Add the butter, cut into small pieces, and rub into the flour until the mixture resembles fine breadcrumbs (**1**).
Add the sugar and mix well.
Beat the egg until smooth. (For the 6 oz pastry ingredients beat the egg yolk and water together until smooth.) Add to the mixture and mix to a stiff paste with a knife (**2**).
Knead lightly (**3**).
Use as required.
NB omit the sugar if using pastry for savoury flans.

What went wrong and why

Speckled	Too much sugar Overcooked
Uneven	Egg insufficiently distributed Uneven rolling
Base risen	Too much water Baked blind without lining Self raising flour used instead of plain

Lining a flan ring
Put the flan ring on a baking tray, and roll out the pastry to about ¼ in. thick, and about 2 in. larger than the flan ring.

Lift the pastry on the rolling pin and put it into the flan ring. Ease it gently into shape (**1**).

Cut off the spare pastry by rolling the pin across the top of the ring (**2**).

Prick the pastry, and add grease-proof paper and baking beans (**3**) or foil (**4**) if you are going to bake 'blind'.

Flaky pastry

	8 oz pastry		12 oz pastry	
plain flour	8 oz	200 g	12 oz	300 g
salt	a pinch of		½ tsp	½ tsp
butter	3 oz	75 g	4 oz	100 g
lard	3 oz	75 g	4 oz	100 g
water to mix	¼ pt	125 ml	½ pt	250 ml

Preparation time about 15 min excluding resting time
Sift the flour and salt into a large bowl.
Cream the fats together until evenly blended. Divide into four.
Add one quarter to the flour and rub in until the mixture resembles fine breadcrumbs.
Add sufficient water to make a slack dough.
Knead lightly until smooth, cover and leave in a cool place for 30 minutes (1).
Roll out the dough to an oblong approximately 5 in wide by 15 in long.
Dot another quarter of the fats over the top two thirds of the dough (2).
Fold the bottom third up over the centre third and bring the top third down over that (3).
Press the edges firmly together to seal (4). Make a mark in the top right hand corner to show the first rolling (5). Cover and leave for 30 minutes.
Turn at right angles and repeat the rolling, dotting with fat and folding process twice more, leaving the pastry to rest in between each rolling.
Roll once more and use as required.

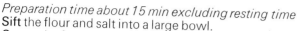

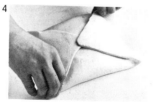

Cream horns
Roll out the pastry into a rectangle, and cut into strips about 1 in. wide(1). Brush one edge of each strip with whisked egg, and wind each around one of the special cone tins (2) beginning at the tip and overlapping slightly. Brush with beaten egg.

Russian fish pie
Bring two opposite corners of the pastry over to the centre of the filling, and brush the edges with lightly whisked egg.
Fold the other corners over so that they overlap slightly¹and make a square(3).Press the edges together (4)and brush with egg.

3 What went wrong and why

Hard	Too much water
	Too much flour used for rolling out
	Too much handling
Fat oozing	Fat too soft
	Edges not sealed during rolling
	Oven too cool
Not flaky	Too much rolling
	Cooled on flat surface
	Fat too warm and soft
Soggy	Oven too hot
	Undercooked

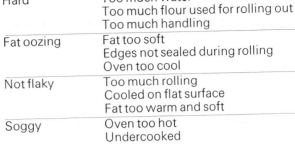

Sausage rolls
Roll the pastry out to a large rectangle, and cut into strips about 4 in. wide.
Roll out the sausage meat into three lengths, place one on each strip of pastry, and brush the pastry edges with beaten egg (5).
Roll each pastry strip in half lengthwise so that it encloses the sausage meat, and press firmly (6).
Brush the tops with beaten egg, cut into suitable lengths, and slash the tops with a knife (7).

Eccles cakes
Put a spoonful of the filling in the centre of each pastry square, and brush the edges with lightly whisked egg white (9). Gather the edges together so that the filling is enclosed (10). Press to seal.
Place the filled pastries seam-side down on a floured board, and roll into 3 in. rounds. Place on wetted baking tray, brush with lightly whisked egg white and make three slashes on the top of each with a sharp knife (11).

Cheese d'artois
Twist each finger of pastry from the centre outwards, so that they look like bows (8).

Puff pastry

	8 oz pastry		1 lb pastry	
plain flour	8 oz	200 g	1 lb	400 g
salt	a pinch of		$\frac{1}{2}$ tsp	$\frac{1}{2}$ tsp
butter	8 oz	200 g	1 lb	400 g
water to mix	$\frac{1}{4}$ pt	125 ml	$\frac{1}{2}$ pt	250 ml

Preparation time about 15 min excluding resting time

Sift the flour and salt into a large bowl.

Add sufficient water to make a soft dough. Shape it into a ball.

Cut the dough half way through in four (**1**), and pull back the centre corners to make a star shape (**2**). Leave covered for 30 minutes.

Meanwhile cream the butter until soft, then shape into a ball.

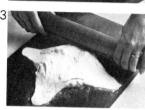

Roll the points of the dough to quarter the thickness of the centre (**3**).

Place the ball of butter in the centre of the dough and overlap the points across the top (**4**).

Roll into an oblong about 6 in by 12 in. Fold in three (**5**), press the edges together to seal and leave covered for 30 minutes.

Turn at right angles and roll into an oblong, repeat the previous processes five more times, leaving to rest in between each rolling.

Use as required.

What went wrong and why

Hard	Too much flour used for rolling out Too much handling
Fat oozing	Fat too soft Edges not sealed during rolling
Not puffy	Too much rolling Fat too warm and soft
Soggy	Oven too hot Undercooked

Vol au vent
Using a 7 in plate as a guide, cut out a circle with a sharp knife. Place the pastry on a damp baking tray, and cut through almost to the base in the centre with a 3 in. cutter. (**1**). Knock up the edges of the case (**2**).

Palmiers
Cut the rolled pastry in $\frac{1}{2}$ in. strips, using a sharp knife (**3**).

Choux pastry

	2½ oz pastry		5 oz pastry	
water	¼ pt	125 ml	½ pt	250 ml
butter	2 oz	50 g	4 oz	100 g
plain flour	2½ oz	75 g	5 oz	125 g
salt	a pinch of		a pinch of	
eggs	2	2	4	4

Preparation time about 20 min
Heat the water and butter until the butter melts; do not allow to boil.
Sift the flour and salt and add to the water and butter. Beat with a wooden spoon until the mixture forms a ball and leaves the sides of the pan clean (1).
Cool slightly.
Add the eggs one at a time (2), beating well after each addition until the mixture is smooth (3).
Use as required.

What went wrong and why

Soft	Flour not cooked enough before adding eggs Oven too cool Undercooked
Not puffy	Eggs not beaten in enough Cooked while beaten in Oven too cool

Eclairs
Fill the forcing bag about ¾ full, and twist the top of the bag (1). Pipe out finger lengths on to a greased tray, starting with the end of the tube touching the tray and lifting it up as the mixture comes out. Cut off with a wet knife (2).

Profiteroles
Spoon the mixture on to a greased and floured baking tray (3).
When cooked, carefully make a slit along the side of each (4).

Suet pastry

	8 oz pastry		1 lb pastry	
self raising flour	8 oz	200 g	1 lb	400 g
salt	a pinch of		$\frac{1}{2}$ tsp	$\frac{1}{2}$ tsp
shredded suet	4 oz	100 g	8 oz	200 g
water to mix	$\frac{1}{4}$ pt	125 ml	$\frac{1}{2}$ pt	250 ml

Preparation time about 10 min
Sift the flour and salt into a large bowl. Add the suet and mix well.
Add sufficient water to make a soft dough (**1**).
Knead lightly (**2**) and use immediately.

What went wrong and why

Heavy	Water not kept boiling
	Topping up pan with cold water
Tough	Too much handling
	Overcooked
Soggy	Undercooked
	Water not kept boiling
Uneven distribution of suet	Suet not shredded finely enough
	Unevenly mixed

Lining a pudding basin
Roll the pastry to a circle which will fit the basin, and cut out a $\frac{1}{4}$ segment (**1**). Place inside the basin, and join the ends so that the pastry fits snugly (**2**). Put the filling in, and roll out the remaining pastry into a circle which will cover the top of the basin. Brush the edge with water.
Lift the pastry on a rolling pin and cover the basin (**3**). Join the edges together firmly (**4**). Cover the basin with greaseproof paper or foil (**5**).

Hot water crust pastry

	8 oz pastry		12 oz pastry	
plain flour	8 oz	200 g	12 oz	300 g
salt	a pinch of		$\frac{1}{2}$ tsp	$\frac{1}{2}$ tsp
water	$\frac{1}{4}$ pt	125 ml	10 Tbs	10 Tbs
lard	4 oz	100 g	6 oz	150 g

Preparation time about 10 min

Sift the flour and salt into a bowl.

Heat the water and lard until the lard has melted. Do not boil.

Make a well in the centre of the flour and pour in the melted lard and water (1).

Mix with a wooden spoon until cool enough to knead lightly with the fingertips (2).

Use as required.

What went wrong and why

Not easy to handle	Too much or too little water Too much flour Too little fat
Collapses when mould removed	Too thin Not cool enough
Hard Cracked	Too much water Insufficient kneading Too little water

Raising a pie
Cut off $\frac{1}{3}$ of the pastry for the top, and reserve ; roll out the rest to a 12 in. round. Flour a 6 in. jar or cake tin, and press it firmly into the centre of the dough (1). Mould the dough evenly up the sides of the jar or tin (2). Cut a piece of foil long enough to go around the pie shape and rather more than twice its depth ; fold in half lengthwise. Wrap this around the pastry, and fold over to secure.

Raising a pie in a mould
Cut off $\frac{1}{3}$ of the pastry for the top and reserve ; place the rest in the base of a 6 in. mould (3). Flatten the dough over the base and up the sides of the mould, pressing firmly (4). Roll out the remaining pastry to fit the top of the pie, place in position, and press the edges together to seal. Trim and pinch edges together (5).

Creamed mixture

	6 oz		8 oz	
butter	6 oz	150 g	8 oz	200 g
castor sugar	6 oz	150 g	8 oz	200 g
eggs	3	3	4	4
self raising flour	6 oz	150 g	8 oz	200 g
salt	a pinch of		a pinch of	

Cream the butter and sugar together until light and fluffy (1).
Add the eggs one at a time, beating well after each addition (2).
Sift the flour and salt and fold into the mixture using a metal spoon (3).
Use immediately.

What went wrong and why

Creamed mixture

Close texture	Insufficient beating Too much flour Oven too cool
Holey texture	Too much raising agent Uneven folding in of flour
Cracked top	Oven too hot
Fruit sunken	Fruit too wet Oven too cool
Cake sunk	Oven too hot Cake moved during cooking Sudden draught

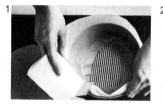

Lining a round tin
Measure around the tin, then measure its depth and add 2 in. Cut a rectangle of greaseproof paper to these sizes, and nick one long edge at intervals of $\frac{1}{2}$ in. Curve this around and slip inside the tin, with the nicked side down (1).

Cut a circle of greaseproof paper a little smaller than the base of the tin, and drop it into place (2).

Shortbread
To finish the edge of shortbread, pinch into the side with the finger and thumb (3).

Whisked mixture

eggs	3 oz		2 oz	
eggs	3	3	2	2
castor sugar	3 oz	75 g	2 oz	50 g
plain flour	3 oz	75 g	2 oz	50 g
salt	a pinch of		a small pinch of	

Put the eggs and sugar into a large bowl and place the bowl over a pan of hot water (**1**).
Whisk the eggs and sugar together with a rotary whisk until the mixture thickens enough to leave an impression of the whisk (**2**).
Sift the flour and salt and fold into the mixture very gently using a metal spoon (**3**).
Use immediately.

What went wrong and why

Close texture	Eggs and sugar insufficiently whisked
	Eggs and sugar heated too much during whisking
	Too much flour
	Flour added too quickly and heavily
Sunk	Too much sugar
	Cake tin moved during cooking
	Cake cooled in draught

Swiss roll

Lining the tin
Measure the length and width of the tin, and add twice its depth. Cut the rectangle of greaseproof paper to this size. Place the paper on the tin, and cut the corners in as shown (**1**). Tuck the cut edges in to fit (**2**), and insert in the tin.

Making the roll
Turn the sponge on to a piece of sugared greaseproof paper. Remove the baking paper from the bottom, and trim the edges with a sharp knife (**3**). Make a cut halfway through the sponge, about $\frac{1}{2}$ in ($1\frac{1}{2}$ cm) from the edge which is to start the roll. Spread with warm jam. To roll up, press in the half-cut edge, and using the paper as a guide, roll firmly (**4**). Leave the paper round the roll for a few minutes to set the sponge, then remove the paper and cool the sponge on a wire rack.

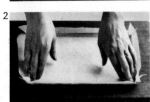

Meringue mixture

	2 oz		3 oz	
egg whites	2	2	3	3
castor sugar	2 oz	50 g	3 oz	75 g
granulated sugar	2 oz	50 g	3 oz	75 g

Whisk the egg whites until stiff and standing in peaks (**1**).
Add the castor sugar and whisk again until thick and shiny (**2**).
Add the granulated sugar and fold in using a metal spoon (**3**).
Use as required.

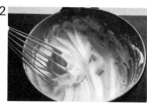

What went wrong and why

Brown and spotty on the outside, soft in the centre	Oven too hot Sugar not properly beaten in
Cracked	Cooked too long Insufficient sugar
Weeping (sugar oozing out from meringues)	Mixture underneath – fruit, puddings-etc. too wet. Too much sugar Sugar not beaten in sufficiently in first stage.

Piping on to rice paper
Fill the bag to about three quarters full, and twist over the top (**1**). Force the meringue through the nozzle into neat stars or whirls (**2**).

Meringue pie topping
Pile the meringue on top of the filling, and shape into peaks with a fork (**3**).

Melted mixture

	8 oz		4 oz	
butter	4 oz	100 g	2 oz	50 g
treacle or syrup	4 oz	100 g	2 oz	50 g
soft brown sugar	4 oz	100 g	2 oz	50 g
bicarbonate of soda	½ tsp	½ tsp	a pinch of	
milk	4 Tbs	4 Tbs	2 Tbs	2 Tbs
plain flour	8 oz	200 g	4 oz	100 g·
salt	a pinch of		a pinch of	

Melt the butter, treacle or syrup and sugar together in a pan (**1**).
Mix the bicarbonate of soda with the milk if used, otherwise sift with the other dry ingredients.
Sift the flour and salt with any other dry ingredients such as spices, fruit etc.
Pour the melted mixture from the saucepan into the dry ingredients, beating well (**2**).
Add the milk mixture, and beat until smooth (**3**).
Use as required.

What went wrong and why

Close texture	Too much treacle
	Too much beating
Sunken	Too much bicarbonate of soda
	Too much treacle
Dry and crumbly	Too little milk

Lining a square or rectangular tin
Measure the length and width of the tin, and add twice its depth. Cut the rectangle of greaseproof paper to this size, cut the corners in as shown (**1**). Tuck the cut edges in to fit (**2**).

Rubbed-in mixture

	8 oz		12 oz	
plain flour	8 oz	200 g	12 oz	300 g
salt	a pinch of		a pinch of	
butter	4 oz	100 g	6 oz	150 g
castor sugar	4 oz	100 g	6 oz	150 g
eggs	2	2	3	3
milk	4 Tbs	4 Tbs	6 Tbs	6 Tbs

Sift the flour and salt into a large bowl.
Add the butter cut into small pieces and rub into the flour until the mixture resembles fine breadcrumbs (**1**).
Add the castor sugar and any other dry ingredients such as fruit, and mix well (**2**).
Beat the eggs with the milk until smooth and stir into the mixture with a wooden spoon (**3**).
Use as required.

What went wrong and why

Close texture	Too much fat
	Too much rubbing in
Dry and crumbly	Too little milk
	Oven too hot
Cracked	Oven too hot
Fruit sunken	Fruit too wet
	Too much liquid
	Oven too cool

Scones
Roll out the dough to about
$\frac{1}{2}$ in thick (**1**). Cut out rounds
with a 2 in (5 cm) cutter (**2**).

Biscuits
Roll out the dough to about
$\frac{1}{4}$ in thick. Prick the dough and
cut out rounds using a 2 in
(5 cm) cutter (**3**).

Bread dough

	3-2 lb loaves		1-2 lb loaf	
plain flour	3 lb	1½ Kg	1 lb	400 g
salt	2 tsp	2 tsp	1 stp	1 tsp
fat	2 oz	50 g	1 oz	25 g
fresh yeast	1 oz	25 g	½ oz	12 g
castor sugar	1 tsp	1 tsp	½ tsp	½ tsp
tepid liquid	1½ pt	750 ml	½ pt	250 ml

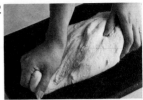

Preparation time about 20 min plus proving time
Cooking time 50 min 425°F (220°C)
Sift the flour and salt into a large bowl. Add the
lard and rub in until the mixture resembles fine
breadcrumbs. Cream the yeast and sugar together
until smooth. Add half the water and mix well again.
Make a well in the centre of the flour, add the yeast
mixture with the rest of the liquid and mix well (**1**).
Knead for about 10 minutes until smooth and
elastic (**2**), shape into a ball (**3**).

Put into a clean bowl, cover and leave in a warm
place until the dough doubles its original size.
Turn on to a floured board and knead the mixture
lightly until smooth.
Divide and shape as required.
Cover the dough in the tins or on the baking tin with
a clean cloth, and leave in a warm place until double
its original size.
Bake as directed.
For additional help see page 73.

What went wrong and why

Close texture	Insufficient water
	Too little kneading
	Not proved enough
	Oven too hot
Coarse texture	Too much water
	Too much salt
	Over proved
	Too little kneading
Broken crust	Not proved enough
	Tin too small
Wrinkled crust	Too much proving
White spots on crust	Left uncovered during proving.

Hot cross buns
Brush the tops of the buns with
milk, and place two strips of
pastry across the top to make a
cross (**1**).

Braided bread
Press the ends together, and
plait the three strips carefully
(**2**).

Chelsea buns
Cut the rolled dough into 1½ in
(4 cm) slices with a sharp knife.
Put the buns closely together
in a shallow baking tray (**3**).

Essential Information

Recipe Instructions

Preparation times
So that the instructions are as helpful as possible, we have included an indication of the time each recipe will take to prepare. This will help you to calculate the length of time needed to complete each finished dish. Of course, the time is only an approximate one, since speeds vary with individual experience.

Cooking times and temperatures
The times and temperatures given with the recipes, although thoroughly tested, are intended only as a guide. You may find that your tastes require variations in the degree of heat or length of time for cooking a recipe. Only experience will show whether some slight adjustments are needed.

Checking the oven temperature
When you are heating the oven and want to find the actual temperature which the oven has reached, while the light is still on, slowly turn the thermostat knob anti-clockwise and note the temperature on the dial when the light goes out.

If you are waiting for the oven to cool and want to find how far the temperature has fallen, slowly turn the knob clockwise and note the temperature on the dial when the light comes on.

Oven shelves
The shelves are always numbered from the bottom to the top of the oven. Mention of 'up' or 'down' refers to the fact that each shelf is reversible. Cooking positions can thus be adjusted slightly, according to the size of dishes, the height of joints, and so on.

Arranging the oven

Before you heat the oven, arrange the shelves in the best positions for the dishes you are to bake.

☐ If the roasting tin is not needed, remove it from the oven. If it is left in it will tend to interrupt the heat distribution. It is not necessary to leave the tin in the oven as a drip tray.

☐ Pies, milk puddings and basins are more easily handled if they are first placed in a shallow baking tray.

☐ Baking tins or dishes should never touch each other or the sides of the oven, as hot air will not be able to circulate freely, and uneven cooking may result.

What goes where

Remember that, while the temperature in the oven varies only a little, the hottest part of the oven is at the top. So use the different positions in the following way.

Top of the oven
Yorkshire puddings, or any food which needs quick and intense heat, should be put at the top of the oven.
If you are using two baking trays – for scones or small cakes – space the shelves evenly in the oven, and reverse their positions half way through the cooking time, or cook the food on the lower shelf for a few minutes longer.

Middle of the oven
Foods which need longer cooking at fairly moderate temperatures – such as fruit or meat pies – should be placed in the middle of the oven.

Bottom of the oven
Large roasting joints or poultry can be placed in the roasting tin on the oven floor, or on one of the lower runners. The floor of the oven can also be used for other dishes such as milk puddings, custards, vegetables or fish.

Abbreviations used

tsp	teaspoon(s)	°C	degrees Celsius
Tbs	tablespoon(s)	oz	ounce(s)
min	minute(s)	fl oz	fluid ounce(s)
hr	hour(s)	lb	pound(s)
°F	degrees Fahrenheit	in	inch(es)
		ft	foot (feet)

Metric abbrevations

g	gramme(s)	kg	kilogramme(s)
ml	millilitre(s)	cm	centimetre(s)

Weights and measures

NB Tablespoons and teaspoons used in recipes refer to **level** measures. A $\frac{1}{2}$ teaspoon is measured lengthwise down the spoon.

If you haven't got scales, the following equivalents can be used as a rough approximation of 1 oz (25 g)

1 level Tbs	granulated sugar, rice, jam, or syrup (use a hot spoon for the syrup)
1 rounded Tbs	castor sugar or currants
2 level Tbs	cocoa, cornflour, dried breadcrumbs, dry mustard, flour, icing sugar, oatmeal, or powdered gelatine
2 rounded Tbs	desiccated coconut, grated cheese, grated chocolate, or ground almonds

Thin liquids, such as water, milk, vinegar or lemon juice can also be measured using the following equivalents as a rough approximation

1 Tbs	$\frac{1}{2}$ fl oz	15 ml
2 Tbs	1 fl oz	25 ml
4 Tbs	$2\frac{1}{2}$ fl oz	65 ml
8 Tbs	5 fl oz	125 ml
16 Tbs	$\frac{1}{2}$ pint	250 ml

Metric measurements

We have used 25 as the basic metric 'unit' in the recipes, in order to simplify the job of conversion from imperial to metric measures, although the **exact** equivalent of 1 oz is 28.35 g.

This means that, when using a recipe with largish quantities (say 1 lb of flour) the end result in metric measurements will be slightly smaller (by about 2 oz, or 50 g)

than that when using the imperial measurements. But it does make it easier to continue using your old kitchen scales, measuring jugs and spoons without having to use a pencil and paper for complicated sums!

Oven temperatures

Celsius (centigrade) oven temperatures are given to the nearest round figure within each recipe, and on the conversion table below. These approximate equivalents have also been calculated to make conversion as easy as possible, and in most cases the celsius figure is roughly half that of the fahrenheit.

Imperial Measurement	Exact Metric Conversion Used For Can Sizes	Metric Equivalent Used In This Book
1 oz	28.35 g	25 g
2 oz	56.70 g	50 g
4 oz	113.40 g	100 g
8 oz	226.80 g	200 g
12 oz	340.20 g	300 g
1 lb	453.60 g	400 g
2 lb	907.20 g	1 kg
1 fl oz	28.35 ml	25 ml
2 fl oz	56.70 ml	50 ml
5 fl oz	141.75 ml	125 ml
$\frac{1}{2}$ pint	283.50 ml	250 ml
$\frac{3}{4}$ pint	452.25 ml	375 ml
1 pint	567.00 ml	500 ml
$1\frac{3}{4}$ pints	992.25 ml	1 litre

Gas to Electricity Conversion Table

°F	225	250	275	300	325	350	375	400	425	450	475
°C	110	120	140	150	160	180	190	200	220	230	240
Gas Mark	$\frac{1}{4}$	$\frac{1}{2}$	1	2	3	4	5	6	7	8	9

Index to recipes

A recipe name appears in italics when it is a variation, or a part of a main recipe.

A recipe name appears in italics when it is a variation, or a part of a main recipe.